INTRODUCTION

The conversation had gotten personal. We were well behind the curtain of my hidden, inner dreams and I was feeling vulnerable and exposed. Not many got to look this deep and this close. Playing with the coffee cup and swirling the remains of my espresso shots to avoid eye contact, I knew his words were true. Deep, deep down, I knew it. But would I *own* those words? Could I? What would that mean for the direction of my life? My career? My whole world?

"Jason, I've known you for years. You are the real deal when it comes to leadership. You lead from your heart with humility and a desire to see people change for the better. By the way, that's rare, and it's a gift. A gift you need to use. People are waiting to follow leaders like you, but you have to be willing to step out in front and give them the opportunity to follow."

I've got to be honest here. I let the cursor blink for several minutes after writing that quote from my friend. I re-read the paragraph several times. Almost deleted it. Reading it makes me feel like I'm wearing a wool sweater with nothing underneath. It's scratchy and abrasive and makes me fidget. It's uncomfortable.

At the same time, what my friend said is true. This journey I've been on the last three years while writing this book has forced me to wrestle with this truth. I spent much of that time running from it, downplaying it or simply hoping it would go away. It didn't. It didn't because it's my truth. Nobody else can claim it, own it and walk in it like me because it was made for me and I for it.

I believe in the core of who I am that we are all wonderfully made—myself included. Admittedly, though, it's much easier for me to talk about your gifts and your truths and your design than it is to turn that spotlight inward and shine it on me. I've asked myself again and again why this might be so. I've learned the answer is mostly fear--fear that I'm not good enough, or original enough or qualified enough. More specifically, I struggled with "you don't have anything to say," and "even if you did have something to say nobody cares or wants to listen." These extinguishers of my fire were on repeat in my head for two solid years.

It's been quite the American Ninja Warrior journey through obstacles of fear and doubt and uncertainty to land this book in your hands. Many times, I was on the verge of quitting. Thing is though, I don't quit. I'm an optimist. Always have been. The glass is never half empty. The sun will always come out tomorrow, and, tomorrow will most certainly be a better day. If there's a cliché about looking at things in a positive light, I probably subscribe to it.

This juxtaposition of my optimism vs. my fear and doubt is why I think the stories in this book are so necessary. If an eternal optimist like me almost quit, what hope is there for the average optimist, or worse, for the pessimist? Right? Well, this is where that "wonderfully made" idea comes into play.

I believe we all have an ember inside of us—created for a purpose and placed deep in our inner being with intention. That ember is **the thing** we were made for. Life, then, is about stirring that ember into a flame to burn against the forces life throws at us to douse it and turn it into a heaping pile of ashes. But this is not a book about how to build the perfect fire or what to use to get it started. No. This is a book all about searching for and uncovering that ember that was lit long before you can remember. That we were each given an ember to tend—to fan, to fuel and to coax into crackling flame. You've seen people who do this well and you admire them. They are the people that jump out of airplanes, run ultra-marathons, sell everything they own and start a business, or try something everyone else says is crazy. They are loved, admired, adored and respected wherever they go because of that *something special* they possess.

And guess what? You possess it too.

Wait, what?!?!? Hold it right there! I can already hear your objections.

DEDICATION

This book is dedicated to Native Ink, Runner Girl, 220 Leadership and Fire Dad and all the other Fire Starters who are mustering up the courage and the grit to just take the next step...and then the next...on the road to finding your fire and fanning your flame. You inspire me with your passion, purpose and persistence.

But also...

To Kristi Gaynor for challenging me to outline the first chapter that unleashed a flood of ideas I didn't know existed.

To Jenni Robbins for telling me to read my own #@%&! book (and SO many other things) when I was close to giving up.

To Becky Fields for saying it like it is and not allowing me to settle.

Most Importantly...

To my remarkable wife—you are a true Fire Starter in every sense of the word—strong, courageous, daring, tenacious, unflappable and loyal. This book and this life I'm chasing and living are simply not possible without you.

Jo Dee,
Thank you for being a constant support on my crazy journey. You are a #firestarter in all you do. So grateful for your friendship. #firstedition Tribe On!
Jason

i

CHAPTERS

I could never do those things.

I'm not good at anything.

I'm too afraid.

Everyone will laugh at me.

I'm not—insert your objection here that has become your mantra for NOT trying.

Look, I'm not saying that all of us are made to be entrepreneurs or sky divers or ultra-marathoners. But what I AM saying is that we are all meant to do **something**. I refer to it as our Original Design or OD. In order to do that something, a hot coal was placed inside and left to us to work into a flame. Problem is, fire is tricky business. If the ground is too wet or the materials are damp, all you get is a lot of smoke. If you only burn kindling, the result is a bright and hot, but unsustainable flame. There's also the question of the type of fire being built. Is it social like a bonfire? Essential like a cooking fire? Industrial like a kiln fire? Life changing like a refining fire?

What's the purpose of your fire?

History shows us that fire was a revolutionary tool in the development of humankind. Cold was transformed by fire's warmth. Darkness was conquered by the blaze of the flame. Fire made the difference, and, if allowed to expire, darkness and cold again prevailed.

Our lives and our world aren't much different to this basic comparison. Become cold and calloused to the world around you, allow negativity and complacency to extinguish your light, your flame, and life becomes a stale and stagnant bumping into one another in the dark. No light. No heat.

You probably know someone that has let their flame grow cold. They are the ones that let life happen to them yet complain all the time about that very life. When you encourage them to do something about it, there is always an excuse for why "it" won't work. If you know one of those people, I also hope you know someone who takes the opposite approach. These are the people that are active in their impact on the world. They work hard to ensure their fire never goes out. They are Fire Starters.

I interviewed four Fire Starters in this book. Their stories are of bravery in the face of news we never want to hear, courage in the face of complacency, and determination in the face of the muck and mire of "that's just the way it is" daily drudgery. They are: Native Ink, Runner Girl, 220 Leadership, and Fire Dad.

Like these four Fire Starters, you have something burning within you too. Really. Not kidding.

What I hope that you'll discover within the pages of this book is that you, too, are wonderfully made -- that you, too, have a gift and unique take on the world that belongs to you alone -- your OD. And that is precisely the point. Some see needs where others don't. Some see investment where others see ruin. Some see a calling where others can't run fast enough in the other direction. The dichotomies are endless. The question is really what are YOU going to do with YOUR ember? Some people will make fun of it. Others will ignore it. But some will embrace it. How do you know who those people are? How they will react? You don't know—until you try.

That brings me to my story. When I first sat down to write this book, I didn't believe my story was worth telling. I sought out others because their stories inspired me much the way I hope they'll inspire you. What I found as I continued to write, though, was that their collective story became part of my own. Over the last three years of writing this book, I have lived it. From the disdain of the status quo in a ten-year corporate career, to a fear of jumping into the unknown when that job was eliminated, to facing those fears that came with striking out on my own, I have ignited the Fire Starter within.

While my journey may look quite different from yours, there is no denying that you **are** on a journey. My hope for you, dear reader, is that you will allow this book to be your *grand excuse*. An excuse that gives you permission on your unique journey to take time for yourself and find that ember in your soul. And once you find, that you will place it on suitable ground, breathe deeply into its core and watch as a beautiful flame comes to life and dances before your eyes. When you see that flame, you will know instantly and inherently that it is good and right. And, at that moment, you can know without a doubt that you have ignited the Fire Starter within.

A quick back story and a challenge...

My nickname in college was The Surgeon. I was not pre-med and had no desire to cut people open for a living. I got this name on a whitewater rafting trip on the Nu River in West Virginia. The Surgeon. Somehow the name fit. I got it because I could build a killer fire—and—keep it burning with surgical precision...

Ok so, maybe that is a bit dramatic, but I was good at starting a fire and keeping it going well into the night and reviving it early the next morning. As I look back on that weekend, I see several similarities between building, starting and sustaining that fire and building, starting, and sustaining my family, my career, my training for a marathon, Fire Starters Inc. The list could go on and on.

I earned the nickname because I would meticulously stack new wood on the fire, get down on my hands and knees and blow until my head felt swimmy. Fire starting is meticulous business and can be quite difficult at times. The right environment along with the right materials are essential to building the perfect blaze.

Therein lies the essence of the FIRE STARTER. There are embers in each of us. Some are white hot and just need the proper fuel and care to burst into flame. Conversely, other embers are at risk of dying out. They need more tending to. More fuel. More oxygen. More stoking.

Whether you are a smoldering ember, a white-hot coal or something in between, your fire is still burning. It may not be a bonfire that draws others around, but with the right fuel and the proper stoking, it could be.

Question. Are you content with burning white hot deep in your gut, but not allowing the flame to catch? Are you content smoldering in a lukewarm existence with only occasional smoke as proof your fire is still burning?

Or, or...

Are you willing to be stoked and poked and have new life breathed in—to transform your smoldering ember into a dancing, crackling flame?

The choice is yours.

This is the **DOing** Page!

At the end of each chapter you'll find a space for you to reflect on what you have read and jot down some action items. One of the core foundations of my company, Fire Starters Inc., is **Inspiration with Action.** Both are necessary for lasting change. I hope these pages will be a place to put down amazing ideas for **Doing!**

Take some time to reflect and jot down 1-3 reactions you have to what you just read and make sure one is active that you will **DO!**

EMBERS

What inspires you? What makes your hands sweat, your heart pound, your stomach churn? When you look around, what do you long for someone to start or change? Or maybe, you've got this *something* that you just can't shake. A need you see you could fill, a service you could provide, a neglected area, a forgotten segment of the population. *Something.* That something? That's your ember. It's got a little heat. It might randomly and sparingly flare up as flame, but then just as quickly disappears.

What's yours?

I can already see some of you shrugging your shoulders. "I dunno."

I can hear others of you moaning with a deep sigh, "I don't **have** an ember.

Yes. You. Do.

Before you read the next paragraph, take five minutes and think about your ember. For some this will come quickly. You've been thinking about it for years. If you've got it, feel free to jump to the next section, called, "A-HA! Moments."

For others, you need to dig at it and really work to uncover it. Some of you have it lodged tightly in that gnawing place just behind your ear. You know it's there because it won't leave you alone, but you never truly acknowledge it. This is your permission to grab hold of your ember, cradle it in your hand, and examine it.

Yes, I still hear the rest of you. You've thrown your hands up, huffed with frustration and grumbled, "I still don't have one!" Yes. You. Do.

Yours, however, is more challenging to find. Yours is buried in the ashes. It's on the edge of being extinguished. Those ashes have been heaped on by (sometimes well-meaning and sometimes not) friends and family. . .

That's a dumb idea!

That will never work!

*Who are **you** to start **that**?*

*What makes **you** so smart?*

Someone else is already doing that. . .

You're too afraid to take that kind of risk. . .

It didn't work before, why would it work this time?

*You've never been good or passionate about **anything**. . .*

Sound familiar? We'll tackle how to overcome that stuff later. But for now, find that ember. Go ahead. Seriously. Look deep, dig it out and take a look. A long look. The ashes have been cleared away. Do you see it? Keep looking.

There it is. It's still glowing. What's it look like? Hold it up. Nice to finally see it again isn't it? Or maybe you are seeing it for the first time.

Okay. Good. Now hold on to it and don't let go! We're just getting started.

A-HA! Moments

I've spent the last twenty years on two continents, in nine different schools and universities, in countless classrooms and board rooms with thousands of students and business executives. There is nothing more soul satisfying than witnessing an **A-HA!** moment spark, ignite and burst into flame. If you're a parent, hopefully you've seen this with your kids. If you're a boss, with your employees. It's that moment when the light comes on and all the pieces snap into place. The universe is aligned, and the angels are singing. Eyes light up. A sense of wonder is in the air. There may be a happy dance or some high fives. (You get the picture.) Bottom line— a spark has found flammable material and the flame is taking hold.

For two decades this has been my addiction. It's intoxicating. I've seen it hundreds of times. There's a physical rush to witness and be a part of these moments. You know what else? It's contagious and it spreads—like WILD FIRE. Age doesn't matter. Gender doesn't matter. Race, socioeconomic status, city, country, cross culture, same culture—none of that matters. There's nothing like an **A-HA!** moment. Every single time I see one, it's like seeing it for the first time.

It will be the exact same when you find your ember. There's a new kind of excitement. A clarity. You'll see things in a different light. You'll have a renewed sense of hope. Dare I say, your desire to settle will begin to wane.

Some of the Fire Starters you will meet in this book describe it as an all-encompassing, all-consuming passion and drive that can't be escaped. Don't worry if you haven't found yours yet—that's why you're reading this book. It's a process that brings excitement and clarity along the way.

M.O.B.

Before I introduce you to some remarkable Fire Starters, allow me to tell you about M.O.B. It stands for My Own Business. For over twenty years I've carted a spiral notebook or manila folder around the world with me, stuffed with random bits of thought, inspiring articles and plans for M.O.B. Plans for *someday...* Plans for *hopefully...*

The last three years have been a realizing of that *someday* and that *hope* as I've written this book and launched my own business. It's been uncanny how I've seen the events I've written about—the milestones, the struggles and the victories of the Fire Starters I interviewed— play out in my own journey. In fact, at a particularly low point when I was pondering giving up, Jenni (who you will meet later) looked at me and said in a not-so-friendly tone, "You need to go home and read your own #^$* book!" And you know what? I did.

Know what else? She was right. M.O.B. MY. OWN. BUSINESS. The pages of this book are M.O.B. Jenni ignited my fire. She took a deep breath and fanned my M.O.B. spark into a flame. Motivation and action define Fire Starters Inc. The transformations you'll discover in this book illustrate the power of motivation and the need for action. It's what I want my clients to experience when they work with me; what I want my kids to learn when they watch me; what I want for you. Wake up and believe it!

#findyourfire, #fanyourflame, #tendyourtribe #chaseyourdream, #beafirestarter, #tribeon

Start following me on social media and it won't take long for you to see any one or a combination of these hashtags in my posts. They are my mantras. The first three are the stages of the Fire Starter's journey. The last three are calls to live radically—calls to get comfortable being uncomfortable. That space on the edge of fear is where great growth happens. But you'll have to take a risk.

I started this chapter asking what inspires you. Let me ask you another way.

~What sets your heart on fire?~

There can be no fanning of a flame that has yet to be discovered. You can't ask a tribe to rally around a vague notion of something you *might* be excited about. You must #findyourfire. Once you do, there's no denying it.

This was the case when our oldest son sat my wife and me down during his junior year in high school and shared his ember with us. Before I tell you what it is, know that your own journey of uncovering your ember may surprise you AND the people closest to you. Such was the case with our son. His ember? The United States Marine Corps.

To say we were surprised doesn't come close. We were gobsmacked.

My wife and I are both educators by trade with MAs in teaching. Her parents were lifetime educators at her high school and we home school all of our children until they reach high school. We have strong beliefs about the advantages of higher education. You can imagine the shock, then, when our oldest son informed us midway through his junior year (at a college prep high school mind you) that he wanted to go straight into the Marine Corps after graduation. My response at the time was something along the lines of, "I'm sorry, but that sounds like you just said you aren't going to go to college." I was right.

So was he—about his ember. The passion and energy he had when he talked about signing up for this Marine Corps adventure was undeniable. He was fully engaged, had done the research, had devised a plan and was itching to get going. Such is the case when you uncover your ember. You plan and dream and research and plan and dream and research. After you do more of that, you start telling people about it. It starts to flow out of you. You can't contain it.

As you are introduced to my Fire Starters, you will see similar themes in their stories. My son told us this Marine Corps adventure was his "calling". As I've seen him excel and thrive in the Corps, his calling seems undeniable. Other Fire Starter's describe their ember in similar ways. It's that thing they would rather try and fail than never try at all. It's what they were made to do—their OD.

Native Ink

For Brandee Gordon, that thing to try and possibly fail at was not the expected path for a promising college athlete. Owner of Native Ink Tattoo (go check her out at www.nativeinktattoo.com) for over twenty-one years, she traded in her softball glove and bat for some paint and a tattoo gun.

Instead of practicing athletics after school every day of her senior year and taking advantage of a sports scholarship, she took $1500 she had been saving plus another $1500 her parents were going to give her as a graduation present and bought in to an apprenticeship at a local tattoo shop. Crazy right? What in the world is a young girl doing in the male-dominated tattoo industry? Doesn't she know that's not allowed? Who does she think she is? Why can't she just go to college and play softball like she's *supposed to*? Doesn't she know she's wasting her potential and throwing away her future? In the Fire Starter's Journey, these questions and those asking them are called "extinguishers." They are such an undeniable part of this journey that they get a whole chapter of their own. For now, let's not allow them to sidetrack us as it relates to Brandee's journey (by the way, they are masters at sidetracking) and get back to her ember.

~Everyone will have an opinion about what you *should* do with your life. Be true to your OD!~

Brandee's response to the extinguishers was a common one among Fire Starters. She said, "So what!?" to them and jumped right in to the tattoo business. Being an apprentice meant mostly doing jobs nobody else wanted to do, like cleaning the tattoo guns, stocking paint and cleaning the shop. This was by no means glamorous, but it gave her an opportunity to observe the business from several angles. During this time, Brandee was learning about something that made her come alive. She was seeing it up close and learning the ins and outs. She was watching clients and watching the artists, smelling the paint, hearing the tattoo guns buzz. The kind of exposure that Brandee experienced isn't something she could have found looking in from the outside or by reading about it in a book. She spent hours every day immersed in the business, and it set her brain on fire with inspiration and creativity. Just that kind of exposure will be an important stage in starting your fire too. Engagement is key. It's never too early or too late to start, and no step is too small.

This is where you can start thinking about your ember and how you can engage it. Can you volunteer somewhere? Can you have coffee with someone who is doing what you are looking for and pick their brain? What can you do to "get your hands dirty"? Send the text, reach out on social media. One thing I know for sure about this part of the process—sitting still and doing nothing will bring you zero results. DO!

When I asked Brandee what advice she would give to fellow Fire Starters, she didn't hesitate. "Follow your passion. Yes, follow your passion!" She was quick to add that doing so is not easy and requires a lot of hard work. Her apprenticeship was drudgery at times. She started at the bottom and the only tattooing she got close to for several months was sketching the ideas clients came in with for the "real artists" to tattoo. All this grunt work, though, was just what she needed to uncover that ember buried deep within her heart.

She knew from the sketches she was drawing that she had some skill. She observed clients as they came through the door of the shop and saw that they were uneasy and didn't really know what to expect. The guys that ran the shop didn't seem to care how or what their clients were feeling and Brandee saw opportunity here to treat her clients differently.

The more she thought about this, the more her ember heated up. She could combine her love for art and her desire to care for people and treat them well into her ideal business model. Finally, this "little girl in a man's world" had the audacity to dream something unheard of in the late '80s. Maybe I'd like to have my own little studio and do this myself... Ember? Check!

As you are introduced to the different Fire Starters in this book, you will learn that their embers have a variety of beginnings and are fueled quite differently from one another. Some are business related, some aren't. Runner Girl was not a tattoo shop apprentice that ditched college for her dream—no, not at all. Hers was an unexpected journey resulting in an unlikely nickname.

Runner Girl

If you run, or have been forced into it by a dog who has mistaken you for lunch, or to catch a toddler who is dashing away like an escaped convict, you probably know what it's like to be out of breath. The world around you stops as you hunker over your knee caps and your chest heaves--all while you command your breathing to come back to earth and be normal again. Good times, right? Believe it or not, there are some who enjoy this feeling after they sprint their last few yards to finish a workout. Such was not the case for Runner Girl (RG).

RG is a stay-at-home, homeschooling mother of three. Busy life. Kids and school and school and kids and laundry and cooking and... I think you understand. As a kid she was active. Walked everywhere. Spent winters on skates. As an adult she was less active, but no less courageous. She started a small business with her husband in their first year of marriage, got her MA in TEFL (Teaching English as a Foreign Language), and had all three of her children naturally, no drugs.

She's tough and smart and works hard with her husband to keep her family moving in the right direction. In the midst of this often-chaotic life, she also found herself to be 50 pounds overweight. She got tired easily. She was uncomfortable when she sat down. She didn't like her body image and was forced by her size to buy clothes she didn't really like. Her husband is a runner and would encourage her to exercise a least a few minutes a day. Start small. Baby steps. RG will herself admit that there were always more excuses than solutions.

I don't have time.

I'm too busy.

I have to get dinner ready.

The kids will interrupt me.

I've never had an "exercise plan" before.

I don't even know where to start.

And then she got the call from the doctor's office. It went something like this:

"Hello, this is Dr. Smith's office. We have your blood test results back from your checkup. Your cholesterol is borderline. No need to take medication *yet*, but make sure to watch your fatty food intake. Cut back on high fats like cream and red meat. The doctor would like you back in three months for a follow up to see how your levels are doing. Call us if you have any questions. Have a nice day." Just another routine call.

Maybe for them.

Up to that point, RG had considered herself relatively healthy. She knew she had gained weight, but the call from the doctor's office made things real in a hurry. Things had somehow gotten out of her control. Borderline? Medication? Oh no! I don't *do* borderline and there is no way I'm taking medication for bad cholesterol. This was a wake-up call that things needed to change. Her weight and lack of physical activity had caught up with her.

She played the message back to herself several times and then played it again for her husband later that afternoon. RG was not okay with any of it. Change had sparked. The **A-HA!** moment took hold and action wasn't far behind.

RG spent the next few days researching the causes of high cholesterol and what could be done to lower it. She had dieted in the past, and even lost a lot of weight through calorie counting and saying no to most of what she wanted to eat. Somehow, though, change had never stuck—until now.

A couple of days after the call from the doctor's office, she told her husband that there needed to be some changes. Her health needed to take priority. RG's research revealed that healthy food choices together with regular exercise should lower her cholesterol. It was time to take charge of her health and her future. No more excuses. The ember was heating up.

When embers heat up there is a desire for change that can no longer be pushed away. The ember's heat demands attention—a nagging to break from the status quo. "The way things have always been" is no longer acceptable. That's what happened with the Fire Starters you're about to meet. This duo (you don't always have to do it alone) left big corporate jobs with promising career paths to work with kids. 'Who does that?' and 'Why would they?', you ask. Meet Joseph and Matthew—a pair of brothers whose leadership is second to none.

220 Leadership

Joseph and Matthew Moheban are brothers roughly two years apart. Their collective **A-HA!** Moment happened early on. They discovered a shared ember. They grew up playing sports and leading school organizations. They will tell you that they were never the fastest, strongest, smartest or most talented on those teams and in those organizations. Despite all that, they both repeatedly found themselves in leadership positions. They explain this recurring phenomenon by what they call their "intangibles"—qualities of good leaders that can be developed, noticed by others, and followed by a group or a team. The brothers have a lengthy list of intangibles that they work on themselves and with their clients, but a short list includes: courage, resilience, fearlessness, collaboration, dealing with failure and character. Joseph and Matthew continually work to refine their own "intangibles" and stress to their clients the need to do the same.

When you meet these two guys, you realize that they don't settle. Even more so, they won't allow those around them to settle either. As Joseph and Matthew grew in their self-awareness, both realized how many of their peers struggled to develop these intangibles, which frequently landed the brothers in leadership positions.

Additionally, Joseph and Matthew's parents (important members of their tribe—more on tribe later) steadily encouraged Joseph and Matthew to disrupt the status quo. In fact, it was their dad's suggestion that led to the eventual birth of 220 Leadership. The name is a numerical representation of what they want their company to stand for—Second to None Leadership. Additionally, Joseph and Matthew's parents (important members of their tribe -- more on tribe later) steadily encouraged Joseph and Matthew to disrupt the status quo. In fact, it was their dad's suggestion that led to the eventual birth of 220 Leadership. The name is a numerical representation of what they want their company to stand for— Second to None Leadership. Joseph and Matthew's dad challenged them to be radical in their approach to summertime employment. What could they create on their own? How could they avoid the typical summer grind of fast food service, lawn care, or house painting? Their unique intangibles kept surfacing, and with them, an astute observation that their peers and others younger than Joseph and Matthew didn't really possess the thought processes or drive that the brothers took for granted. They had a deep desire to teach students how to recognize and develop these, and in the process help them grow into more effective leaders. The ember started heating up. At ages 18 and 20, the Moheban brothers wrote a curriculum to make the intangibles tangible and teach middle school kids how to have "the edge." Their first summer camp called The Edge was born. Fifteen kids attended that camp during its first summer. That initial group leant momentum to their vision and the following year the program was picked up by their township and tripled in size from the first year!

Stop here for a moment and consider what the Moheban brothers accomplished. At 18 and 20, they saw a need and had a hunger to satisfy it with something they created! They weren't just mowing lawns or flipping burgers or wasting time playing video games. There's nothing wrong with these jobs or activities in themselves, but they're...normal...expected. They stepped out of the ordinary. They threw off the mundane to create something new and exciting. They chose leadership—a word even some business experts have trouble categorically defining—and created programs, curriculum and activities around it.

Who does that for a summer job? Who leaves "dream jobs" to "pay it backwards" to a younger generation? Joseph and Matthew did, and for now, that's all you need of their story to see how your ember can spark and give life to a new idea, a different way. That thing you think everyone else knows? They don't. That strategy you've employed for years that keeps you organized and productive? The world doesn't know it. Even, if they do, they could surely use a reminder. Your ember is as unique to you as Joseph and Matthew's is to them. It's time to start doing something with it!

Your **A-HA!** moment could be realizing that you have something others don't, could be test results, or could be an observation of a need to fill. It's different for everyone and that's what's so exciting. Regardless of what it is, when you finally experience the **A-HA!** moment with your ember, you are on your way to igniting the blaze.

I don't want to skip over this too quickly. I have recently started asking my audiences, "What makes your heart catch fire and come alive?" And I've discovered something shocking. Most people have no idea! I used to think that this was because people were afraid to ask the question. While I believe that fear is a major contributing factor, I've also realized that we simply don't take time to slow down from the "everyday stuckedness" and ask that question. There is a whole host of reasons for this, and that's probably the topic for another book altogether. But as you are reading **this** book, and asking yourself **this** question, you might be afraid. Afraid of the question itself or the answer to it. Or maybe both. You may also just be so busy running or so mired in the stuck that you haven't even asked yet.

Regardless of the reason, the question must be asked. So, if you glossed over it the first time, let me ask you again.

What makes your heart catch fire and come alive?

Your answer to that question could be the very thing the world has been waiting for and so desperately needs.

The **DOing** Page

Take some time to reflect and jot down 1-3 reactions you have as a result of what you just read and make sure one is active that you will **DO!**

Extra **DOing** space in case you need it.

OXYGEN

When I was ten years old, my boyhood buddies and I were exploring some trails at the end of our street. We found a tree with a limb that looked like a parallel bar. To a group of ten-year-old boys, it was an obstacle in our "Special Ops Training." We would jump from a stump, catch the limb, swing our legs as high as we could and let go at the apex of our swing. I was third in line. I climbed up on the stump, jumped, caught the branch and was swinging toward the perfect dismount when my hands slipped off the branch and I landed flat on my back. The impact completely knocked the wind out of me. I could not catch my breath. This was a first and I freaked out! I felt like I was in a vacuum. I opened my mouth, but no sound came out. I had no oxygen. I kept pointing to my open mouth to show my friends that I couldn't breathe. I needed oxygen. For a few fearful moments, I really thought I was going to die. Eventually, my breathing returned to normal and the moment passed, but I've never forgotten the terror I felt when I was breathless.

Oxygen is quintessential. Without it, we die. Duh.

Embers are no different.

They can snuff out and turn cold when there's no oxygen. Conversely, a fresh burst of oxygen can take a dying ember from flicker to flame in an instant.

In 1991, Ron Howard used this phenomenon of smoldering ember to blazing flame as the title for his blockbuster success, *Backdraft*. A backdraft happens when all the oxygen has been sucked out of a room, but an ember is still smoldering. There's still heat present, but the fire can't breathe and grow. Sometimes firefighters experience this (as they did in the movie) when they bust down a door where an ember has been slowly burning. The sudden burst of oxygen mixes with the heat of the ember and can end in a pretty fantastic explosion.

Remember The Surgeon? Being The Surgeon was dirty business. Once I had exposed the hot coals, I had to add some fuel around them that would easily ignite as I gave the fire the Big Bad Wolf treatment. This required getting on my hands and knees with my face just inches away from the coals, filling my lungs to capacity and huffing and puffing on the glowing embers. Cooled embers meant more exertion, more blowing, more work. If the ground was damp or the fuel was wet or both, the work down on my knees took a lot longer. Those bouts typically ended with me inhaling some ash, marking up my face with soot and trying to regain my balance from an oxygen-deprived head rush.

If the embers were still fairly hot, with a few puffs the kindling caught fire and, 'Voila!' FLAME! This was no backdraft, but the embers' immediate response to a fresh burst of oxygen was unmistakable. Heat. Light. Flame.

~Not all embers are the same.

Some require more work than others.~

As you breathe oxygen into your ember, you'll notice a change. First, a glow, albeit brief. You'll feel the slightest bit of heat. Something in you will spark and begin to catch fire. Remember, fire needs constant tending. As it grows you will need to keep breathing life into it. Always more fuel. Always more oxygen. Fanning the flames, as it were, is your responsibility as a Fire Starter.

Don't get discouraged if you get light-headed from all the huffing and puffing. Don't get discouraged if you don't feel like anyone is paying attention and you are doing all the heavy lifting. This is **your** work and **your** ember. Remember? You were made for this. You might get discouraged. You might think about quitting. **DON'T QUIT!** Who will do this work if you don't? Nobody.

I believe this with my whole heart. If you do not pay attention to this ember…if you don't do the work to fan it into a flame…you are depriving the world of something unique that you were born to give. Give it!

We idolize the Steve Jobs, Oprah Winfrey, Bill & Melinda Gates types. The ones who 'made it.' The ones who, in our minds, are bigger and better. They're empire makers. What if they had quit?

Let's bring it closer to home. I almost quit writing this book. I was so close. I felt stupid and under qualified. *You call yourself an author? You can't write! Do you know how many people are going to laugh at this book? By the way, they'll only laugh if they get a chance to read it which means you'll have to publish it, which you and I both know will never happen!* Every day, the same story. Endless repeat. Over and over again. My mind was a landfill full of head trash. Discouraging? Absolutely.

Until...

That huffing and puffing produced heat...eventually. For months, I got up to write while it was still dark outside. There were days when it felt like crawling out of a warm tent to an icy campsite on all fours to breathe fresh oxygen into that ember. Some mornings it was messy business, lots of huffing and puffing barely producing anything even resembling a flame. Other days, coaxing that flame out of the ashes came almost effortlessly. All this to say, again, **stay at it**. Put in the time and the effort when nobody else is looking. Build the habit of consistency. Hone the craft. Do the work.

Native Ink's artistic ember was already burning, but it took her mom breathing oxygen during her growing up years to fuel the flame. She recalls her mom saying again and again:

A closed mouth doesn't get fed.

No question is a dumb question.

You have to try because if you fail, you fail. Who cares? But if you succeed, then awesome!

Can you feel the fresh air of encouragement blowing in? Brandee's parents were actually the ones who found the tattoo parlor where she originally apprenticed. They found the owner's card in a motorcycle shop, took it home to Brandee and encouraged her to reach out to the owner. Pure oxygen.

RG got her oxygen in the form of a jolting call from the doctor's office delivering one word: BORDERLINE. Sometimes our everyday routine needs to be radically turned upside down to make us realize how truly uncomfortable we are in our discomfort. We have lived in it for so long that the discomfort becomes normal.

If you've ever watched the show *Hoarders*, you've seen some disturbing, real-life examples of this play out. I remember watching one episode featuring a woman living in a house overrun by cats. The only "open" space in her home was her living room. There was a very narrow, windy path through rooms piled high with junk on every side (and cats everywhere) leading to this 5X5 area where there was a TV and a recliner that was basically a collection of springs on a frame that she used as a bed. At the end of the show, her house had been cleaned out, the cats taken to an animal shelter and a proper bed donated. She was in tears as she thanked those who had helped her in this process. During the post interview she said something that still sticks with me. "I lived that way for so long, alone except for my cats, that I came to believe this misery was normal."

Whether your current reality is misery, discomfort, or something in between, your current reality does not need to be your future reality. You may have gotten a "borderline" call that paralyzed you. You may have worked for an abusive boss for so long that, like the cat lady in *Hoarders,* you have come to accept that misery as normal. It may have been so long since you've seen your ember, that you fear it's gone forever. I promise you it's not. It's there. It's just in serious need of oxygen. How can I be so sure? Because I've seen the **A-HA!** moment spark in so many like you who are stuck in the mire of your current reality. I've seen it in my own life.

I've also had the privilege of seeing **220 Leadership** work their magic in workshops, and seen participants sit up and take notice of their ember as the fresh oxygen pours in. **220 Leadership** took their normal and made it available to others in those "intangibles." Their oxygen showed up in encouragement from their parents, reception from the school for their program, and feedback from participants. One experience led to another experience. They didn't quit. They didn't give up and the fire kept growing. Oxygen adds momentum that adds oxygen that adds momentum…

I live in Indiana where it gets in the upper 90s in the summertime with 90% humidity. In a word, miserable! Some evenings, though, when a storm has blown through, it brings a fresh reprieve. The heaviness is gone. The air is lighter, and it no longer weighs and hangs like a hot, wet towel. That's what this fresh dose of oxygen is like to our embers. When oxygen is added to an ember, when new life in the form of fresh air reacts with that thing that is already in the process of slow burn, the ember reacts—sometimes like a backdraft. Other times, there's a shift in the flame. It grows and gets hotter and as long as new oxygen is being breathed in, the flame will continue to grow.

This happened with the Fire Starters in varying ways and it happened with me. Let me be crystal clear here. If you don't feed your ember, it will die. Huffing and puffing can be dirty business, but it is *necessary* business. It's *your* business. You are responsible for tending this ember and making sure fresh oxygen arrives in consistent and regular doses. It's tempting here to blame lack of effort on past hurts, past failures, lack of time, or whatever else you are used to blaming. I'm amazed at how creative people can be to find excuses for not doing the work. Stop making excuses. Fan the flame. The ember *will* respond. The flame *will* grow, and the heat *will* intensify.

The **DOing** Page

Take some time to reflect and jot down 1-3 reactions you have to what you just read and make sure one is active that you will **DO!**

Extra **DOing** space in case you need it.

SMOKE

Where there's smoke, there's fire.

True.

Sometimes. . .

Fire Dad

Fire Dad is a veteran fire fighter of eighteen years with a wife and four boys at home. I was originally interested in his expertise as a fire fighter to make sure I understood fire correctly to present my facts without error. Fire Dad and I have known each other for a while and he happily agreed to answer my questions while also giving me a tour of his firehouse. I wasn't expecting to include him in this book, but after our interview, it was clear he was not only a fire fighter, he was also a perfect example of a Fire Starter.

I asked him to walk me through some of the science of fire and the relationship between smoke and fire. Turns out that smoke *often* means fire, but it's not a guarantee. He introduced me to something called the fire triangle. The diagram[1] sums it up. For a fire to burn, all three sides of the triangle must be equally present.

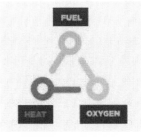

Let's break this down using a camp fire analogy. Picture the scene. The sun is setting, dinner has been cooked on the camp stove, the dishes have been cleaned, and the fire has been meticulously constructed in a pyramid shape. You made sure to bring lots of newspaper for easy fuel, the kids gathered twigs for the kindling, you are proud that you remembered your axe for splitting a few logs into smaller ones that would catch fire quickly, the s'more ingredients are all laid out, and everyone is jumping around saying, "Light the fire!" "Light the fire!"

"Honey, where are the matches?" you shout across the camp site.

"You packed them!" she shouts back.

Panic! You rifle through your gear, ransack the car. Nothing. You search the corners of your pockets *again* hoping that a lighter has magically materialized, but the search is hopeless. All that work going into building the fire is an exercise in futility if there is no heat source to ignite the flame.

In fact, if any of the three sides of the triangle aren't present, there's no fire. No fuel (wood, paper etc.)? No fire. No match, no lighter? No fire. Got match and wood but no oxygen? No fire. All three *must* be present. When they are, smoke is typically not far behind. However, Fire Dad pointed out that it is possible to have smoke but no flame. While it is true that many fires produce smoke like what we see on the news, I learned that smoke occurs when there is incomplete combustion. Simply stated, there is not enough oxygen to burn the fuel completely.[2]

So, what does this look like for your ember? You have all the sides of the triangle present. Remember, the premise of this book is that you have an ember inside of you. The triangle has been formed. Your job is to make sure that all three sides of it work in harmony. Heat. Fuel. Oxygen. Put those all together and you get a fire that starts to smoke and that's a sure sign of a good fire, right? Not necessarily. Fire Dad taught me that there can be lots of smoke, but no actual flame.

Hmm...could this mean that some of us who thought we were tending our ember well are just, uh, blowing smoke?

If you search the term "blow smoke," you'll find several origins and uses. One of the more intriguing uses is to blow smoke up someone's backside to revive a drowning victim. Look it up! As you may imagine, research proved this ineffective... Today, to blow smoke means, "To say things that are not true in order to make yourself or something you are involved with look better than it is."[3]

This may or may not be you, but I personally see Fire Starters do this all the time. Have you ever talked to someone about their passion and notice how their eyes light up? Their posture changes and their voice gets more animated. Then, you ask them about what they do for a living and they (often) transform into a living Eeyore from a Tigger right before your eyes. There's no life, no excitement, no joy. Poof! Cloud of smoke.

You try to pull them back out of the cloud. Why aren't you doing *that*? When are you going to get started on *such and so*? What are you waiting for!?!

Now comes the smoke. Tell me if any of these sound familiar:

Well, I'm getting ready to sit down and put pen to paper on that. . .

I've got some plans to get that started next quarter after things settle down a bit...

I've gotta get together with some thought leaders on this idea I have. . .

As soon as A, B, and C are done, then I'll have time for XYZ...

I've got it all clear in my head, I've just got to sit down and flesh it out.

Smoke can be a sign of fire or a defense mechanism.

I've seen both.

When Fire Starters blow smoke, they are trying to hide in the cloud. They hope that others' eyes will sting enough, and they'll cough enough that they'll have to go away. It's truly a smoke screen. Here's the problem with smoke screens. They require a lot of energy to maintain. Consequently, if we spend our time and energy blowing smoke, there's no oxygen left over.

I blew a lot of smoke myself while writing this book. I told people for a couple of years that I was writing a book. That was a little risky, but still pretty safe. As long as I was *writing* the book, I didn't have to produce anything for anyone to read. It was a work in progress, and I was busy in the process of writing the book. See what I was doing? I was hiding in the process. I was writing, I was making progress, but really I was mostly hiding. As I got closer to the end of the book I started panicking a little bit. What if it's terrible? What if nobody reads it? I Cough, cough. Eyes watering.

I was caught in the smoke.

Most firefighting authorities will tell you this: Smoke kills more than flame. It is full of toxins that fill the lungs and do tremendous damage. Smoke is also incredibly disorienting to victims of a fire as well as firefighters. As a result, people trapped in a fire can't see and can't find their way out of a burning building. Imagine, the smoke is burning your eyes as you cough wildly and try to breathe. It's all in vain as every breath fills your lungs with more smoke and there is less and less oxygen. There is little hope for survival, then, if you are stuck in the smoke, disoriented and the building you are in is engulfed in flame.

Fire Dad, whose name is Dave, is 6 feet tall and weighs 250 pounds. He's solid. His upper body is evidence of his time in the gym. He's also a bit of a teddy bear... That said, I wouldn't want him bear hugging me. He's a "man's man." He's a firefighter. He knowingly and voluntarily walks into burning buildings without anything to put out the fire! He walks in with a glorified crowbar to beat down walls and windows to rescue people and bring them out of the smoke. Oh, and did I mention that when he dons his gear to walk into those burning buildings that it adds another 70 pounds to his frame? Seriously, the guy's a beast.

Fire Dad works on a squad. This means he works within a ladder company that carries hoses and ladders, but he and a partner also work separately and use an SUV to respond more quickly to calls that don't require a fully equipped engine. His tool of choice is a haligan bar. He showed it to me when I visited him at the firehouse. It's basically a 3-foot-long, 20-pound crowbar that has a metal V at one end and a pick axe at the other. So, when Fire Dad walks into a burning building, he's not carrying a hose or an extinguisher. He's carrying a halligan bar. He uses this to smash in windows, pry open doors, bust through walls, or clear pretty much whatever else stands in his way as he goes room to room looking for people trapped in the blaze.

He likes working on a squad. Where the engine will make three to four runs a day, the squad will make ten. He also likes the variety. Their fire house is downtown, so they go on several medical runs as well as fire emergencies a week. Though they go on separate runs from the engine, they also accompany the engine when there is a major emergency call. He recalled a run where he and his partner were so busy doing different jobs putting out a fire, that they went through three air tanks each. They spent their first tanks on search-and-rescue going room to room looking for survivors. Suppression work is what we often see on the news with firefighters spraying water on a structure to put out the fire. Fire Dad and his partner depleted their second tank on suppression work. Once a fire has been suppressed, firefighters go to work on overhaul— the job of exposing all the structural components of the house to make sure the fire is out. This was their last job of the night and took one more tank of air to complete.

Fire Dad not only taught me about smoke and its dangers, he also taught me about the brave men and women who willingly walk into the burning buildings looking for those who are trapped and disoriented.

When he talks about what he does--about rescuing people and bringing them to safety, you hear love for his vocation. It's obvious in his tone and his excitement as he recounts different runs he's been on. He enjoys the variety and surprise that comes with being on the squad. As we talked, we were interrupted by the squawk of the dispatcher over the PA. While we waited for the announcement to end, I looked out at the trucks I got to crawl through and the tools I got to hold as Fire Dad explained the function of each. I thought about how exciting it must be to be in a vocation with so much variety and answer a "hero's calling" at the same time. My mind drifted a bit as I thought about racing through traffic to the next great adventure. The dispatcher's announcement ended, and Fire Dad surprised me with his next statement. This—the smashing down of walls and rescuing people from burning buildings—this isn't his ember.

I'm sorry, what!?!?! I wasn't expecting this. Growing up, I was certainly among those boys who wanted to be a firefighter. I wanted to ride on the ladder truck, wear the gear and the helmet, sling an axe over my shoulder and search burning buildings for survivors. Fire Dad is living my boyhood dream! In fact, part of his job is to go to schools in his gear and talk about fire safety—all the while fueling that dream of kids like me to one day be like him. I sat there stunned as he went on to explain his true ember.

"I'm *good* at my job," he explained. He's been doing this for a long time and likes to learn and has learned a lot about fighting fires and search-and-rescue. People can count on him in a crisis. Everybody knows it. He further described other members of his team who are, in his words, *great* at their job. As he ended that narrative, he reiterated how much he *likes* his job, but it's not his passion. Before I had a chance to ask, he answered my unspoken question. "My passion is being a husband to my wife and a father to my four boys." And just like that, I witnessed the physical and emotional shift that happens when people tap into what sets their hearts on fire. Fire Dad's eyes got big, his posture changed as he sat up and leaned in and his voice came alive with excitement.

He recounted how he feels about his calling as a dad and how important it is to be there for his wife and kids. He and his wife homeschool their four boys. They decided that Dave would take fewer shifts at the firehouse so he could be home more with his family and be more involved in homeschooling. Their decision has not come without sacrifice. They are on a tight budget and the boys are learning to eat some things that they didn't have to when Dave had more shifts. In Dave's eyes, though, the sacrifice is well worth it. His family is his ember and he is working hard to build a fire that will burn well into the lives of his future grandchildren.

There's no blowing smoke here. This is sustainable flame. No "*I'm thinking about* taking fewer shifts at work," no "*One of these days* I'll work less and spend more time with the wife and kids." None of that. He's not getting ready to do something or putting a plan together. Instead of blowing smoke, he's stoking the flame. The fire triangle is in full effect. His wife and kids agree.

Pay attention to your fire triangle and the smoke it produces.

Native Ink's ember smoked as she took the apprenticeship at the tattoo parlor. It smoked a bit more when she looked around and saw a gap she could fill, and it burst into flame when she struck out on her own.

At first, Runner Girl's fire triangle was lopsided. Any smoke from her fire was a defense to keep people away. But when all the sides of her fire triangle aligned, she could no longer hide in smoke. Instead, the smoke proved her ember was growing into the flame it was meant to be.

As you tend your own ember and get the sides of your fire triangle in proper alignment, life will begin to change in undeniable ways.

This isn't usually something that happens overnight. You've probably witnessed someone struggling to build a camp fire. There is a lot of smoke and a lot of red-faced huffing and puffing while on all fours, but not a lot of actual fire. With time and tending and the right combination of the fire triangle, flame can be coaxed from the ember.

I was stuck for a while.

For those of you looking for a quick fix to your "stuckedness", or the skies to open up and magically tell you what "it" is, I have some bad news. This Fire Starter thing—it takes work. Hard work. And dedication. And, this part is extremely important, so pay attention! It takes a Tribe—and that's good news because it means you aren't in this alone.

The **DOing** Page

Take some time to reflect and jot down 1-3 reactions you have to what you just read and make sure one is active that you will **DO!**

What a welcome sight it must be to someone trapped and disoriented in a burning building to see a fire fighter bust i

TRIBE

I belonged to a fraternity in college. Initiation night was special. All the members were expected to attend as we welcomed the new members into the brotherhood. There were many traditions on that night, but my favorite was when the ceremony ended. We would all stand in a circle with our arms around each other's shoulders and sing the song, "He Ain't Heavy, He's My Brother." Make fun if you want. Even today that song sparks powerful memories of those initiation nights.

What I remember most is catching the knowing eyes of my friends in that circle as we sang. Some would smile, others would wink, and some would just give you "that look." That look, the smile and the wink all said one thing—"I got your back." They were my tribe. They were advocates, advisers, accountability partners, aiders and abettors. They listened to my crazy ideas, and indulged my attempts to see the bigger picture, chase life and bust up the status quo. Even if they didn't completely believe in *it*, they believed in *me*.

They believed in *me*. Who believes in you? Do you know? Do you pay attention to the things that your colleagues, family members, childhood friends, fellow faith community members and those that surround you daily say? Have you asked them? What a difference my tribe has made in my journey as I wrote this book and left my 10-year corporate career to go full-time running my business, Fire Starters Inc.

My tribe has shown up for me in a very real way—consistently and on purpose. You may be asking what this looks like. How did they show up? What did they do to support me? First, they allowed me to be vulnerable and lean on them when I was doubting myself. This solo-preneur gig can be as lonely as it is exciting. There's no team to lead, no boss to report to, no shareholders to hold you accountable. This all makes it really easy to get in your head and stay there. As a result, bad days can be very bad and the WhatIfAbouts can take their toll. You're going to see this term, WhatIfAbouts, throughout the rest of this book. Here's a definition:

WhatIfAbouts (WIAs) (noun)—1. The conscious and unconscious space we get stuck in that is full of fear and doubt and precludes/prevents/blocks/obstructs our forward progress. 2. The head trash that plays on repeat about past problems, current short-comings and future failures.

I post quite a bit on social media—especially on LinkedIn and Instagram. If my tribe notices that I haven't posted for several days, I get text messages saying things like, "Hey B., haven't seen you post lately and haven't talked to you for awhile. Hope things are going well, let me know what you need." Or, "Hey I thought of you today when I saw X and want to encourage you to keep doing what you're doing. It matters." In this way, they are like Fire Dad with the haligan bar breaking down the door of a burning building and pulling me out of the smoke. They are pulling me out of a place that had me a little lost and disoriented.

By the same token, I can send an email or text message saying I'm struggling because a big potential client hasn't responded or because one said no, or three said no in one week. I'm allowed to lay it out there and talk about being pissed, stressed, anxious or whatever emotion comes along as I figure out what it means to own a business where I am the brand and I write the content. I need the perspective of people who know me and have known me, but also the perspective of people that may know me less well yet are still doing what I'm doing to make a living. You've probably heard the quote about it taking a village to raise a child, right? Well, it takes a Tribe to care for one another. As I look back into history, I see that I am not alone in this belief.

The writer of the book of Hebrews in the New Testament wrote, "And let us not neglect our meeting together as some people do, but encourage one another..."[4] It's important to live among and with others who see you and know you. We're not meant to walk our paths alone. Another often quoted nugget of wisdom from King Solomon in the Old Testament states, "Two are better than one because when one falls the other can help him/her up and though one may be overpowered, two can defend themselves. A cord of three strands is not quickly broken."[5] One application that resonates with me as it relates to the concept of Tribe, is that none of us should be on this journey alone. I'm not saying you *can't* do this alone, but I am saying that your chances of failure *increase significantly* when you are by yourself. Conversely, though, your chances of failure decrease *even more significantly* when you are surrounded by your Tribe.

In many ways, your tribe is like Fire Dad and his whole firefighting company. They have skills to rescue people from burning buildings. They each have particular skills and tools to do their jobs. They work together as a team and lean on each other for support. Your tribe should be filled with people who can rescue you when you are lost in the smoke and catch you when you need to jump to safety. You need your tribe and they need you.

The world tries to tell us differently. Hollywood has long been obsessed with superheroes. Their ability to go it alone and carry the weight of the world solely on their shoulders is showcased and touted as admirable. Admitting weakness is, well, weak. This bleeds over into parenting, traversing adolescence, working, you name it. In the U.S. especially, we love to offer help and assistance, but loathe being on the receiving end of aid—especially on an individual level. Think about it. When was the last time you asked for help or let someone help you? Yes, I hear some of you trumpeting your list of accomplishments and how well you have done on your own. OK, maybe you've done well on your own. It's possible. But let me ask you this. How's your stress level? How's your health? How many medications are you taking to "keep things under control?" One more thing. If you want to know if you have this superhero approach to life, just ask your Tribe!

Before you can ask them, though, you need to know who is in your tribe. Think about it for a minute. Who do you spend your time with?

Who do you celebrate with? Who do you grieve with, go to for help or encouragement? Who do you pick up the phone and call when something amazing happens? Or something tragic? This is your tribe.

Jim Rohn was a motivational speaker all over the globe and is most often credited for saying (among other things), You are the average of the five people you spend the most time with. If indeed this is true, don't you want those five people to be inspiring, passionate, thoughtful, caring, curious and wise? Don't you also think it's a good idea to take an inventory of your tribe to make sure you have the right people playing the right roles? Yeah. Me too!

I'm excited for you to work through what I call the Tribal Inventory that I created while writing this book. It's based on interviews with hundreds of people talking about the people they surround themselves with on the daily. While I was creating this Tribal Inventory, I released it to some of my own tribe to survey their tribes. The feedback revealed two key areas of importance regarding their tribes. They identified existing tribe members, those they needed and those who needed to go. They also recognized they should have taken the inventory a long time ago.

Before digging deep into this notion of tribe, study the list and its definitions below. As you do, think of people in your life who fit a particular role's description and write their names at the bottom of each description. There may be one person you know who fits more than one role description. You may have some roles where several people come to mind. Still others may not have any names. That's OK. This is your initial pass of your Tribal Inventory. First, we figure out who you have under each role. Don't worry so much about how well they are fulfilling the role. For now, let's explore the definitions of the seven quintessential members of a Tribe and who you have as members.

For a free download of the complete Tribal Inventory, go to www.firestarterstribe.com and click the button promoting this tool.

Listener—This is the person that you spill your ideas to in a spastic and chaotic stream of consciousness. They follow you down every rabbit hole and take all the detours along the way. They may ask clarifying questions to understand you better and to help you build clarity as you think out loud. But mostly, they are quiet. This tribe member doesn't offer advice or try to solve for X or Y or even Z. When you are out of breath at the end and ask, "Ya know what I mean?", they nod their head yes with knowing certainty. Mostly though, they... just...listen.

These are my Listeners: _____

_____

Dreamer—This tribe member loves to start sentences with, "What if..." They take your idea and push it to the edge of possibility. Their ideas are larger than life and often fuel your own ideas to grow into spaces you wouldn't dare go on your own. We walk away from our time with them on an adrenaline rush and our minds are full of new and exciting ideas. Typically, they don't have any ideas on the *practical* and that's okay because their job is to DREAM. BIG!

These are my Dreamers: _____

_____

Devil's Advocate—An essential member of the tribe that is often avoided—on purpose. They are also the most misunderstood. They poke holes in plans and dreams because they can't help it. Their minds are just wired that way. They are drawn to all the scenarios that will never happen and all the reasons your dream is going to go up in a cloud of smoke. They aren't trying to rain on your parade, they simply want the best for you and this is their way of showing it. Timing for when to engage the Devil's Advocate is key. Bringing them in at the beginning can be a dream killer, but bringing them in once the plans are drawn out can be a solid dose of necessary reality.

These are my Devil's Advocates: _____

_____

Organizer—Identifying and ordering priorities is this member's specialty. They thrive on details and "the little stuff" that are necessary to make reality, well, reality. They take the chaos of the swarm of ideas and deliver it in a well-organized step-by-step package. They think about sequencing and the necessary resources of both people and time. "Oh yeah, I didn't think about that! " is our looped response when meeting with them.

These are my Organizers: _____

_____

Catalyst—They throw down the gauntlet or give you that extra push over the hill. However you want to describe the catalyst, they are the ones that give legs to that "next step." They give you an assignment and a deadline and assure you they will be there to check on your progress, and then they show up and check on your progress! In fact, they're a little obsessive/borderline annoying about it, but we love them for it!

These are my Catalysts: _____

_____

Connector—This tribe member could be beneficial multiple times throughout the process. They have a network and aren't afraid to use it. Their comments after listening to you might include, "You know, you need to talk to this person" or "You should meet with my friend who does. . . " They get excited when tribes get connected because it grows their tribe and connections, and that's what connectors are all about.

These are my Connectors: _____

_____

Expert--The expert is the one who has already arrived at the place you are trying to go. They are mentors. They have the inside track on where you are going. They know the life hacks to accelerate your growth and success, but might strategically hold back certain pieces until you are ready, thus enabling you to learn from the experience yourself. They are simultaneously your biggest fans and your biggest challengers. You leave every conversation with the expert feeling confident and energized to take your next step.

These are my Experts: _____

_____

All these roles are essential in your tribe. They all play a part and you need every single one of them. Some of these roles *can* be filled by the same people. I find it best, however, to have separate individuals for each role. This helps create and maintain a diversity of skills, beliefs and approaches that will ultimately benefit you as you lean on your tribe in times of need.

Since officially launching Fire Starters Inc., I have found it crucial to have several connectors and experts in different areas of business. I have intentionally focused on financial services, HR, health care and education as industries I want to work in. Because my connectors in financial services don't typically have connections in education and vice versa, it's been so beneficial to have several people filling this role for me.

Your particular needs are likely very different from mine—as they should be. You might have one or two listeners compared to five connectors, or five dreamers (that could be dangerous) compared to just one or two devil's advocates. The combinations are many. You may also have other roles according to your own purpose, but I find that these roles are must-haves.

A Tribal Inventory consists of three distinct stages: Admire, Hire and Fire. Each stage is essential and should not be skipped. I take all my coaching clients through a Tribal Inventory. The outcomes and reactions are as varied as the people filling out the inventory. One client who filled it out told me she finally understood why she was so depressed and never felt like her ideas took off the way she wanted them to. Her inventory revealed **FIVE** Devil's Advocates and **ZERO** Dreamers! Another client I was anxious to hear from after she completed hers told me she was shocked at the results. Turns out she had **NO** tribe. "No wonder I'm so exhausted and feel so lonely most of the time," she said. I looked at the Tribal Inventory and realized I was ALL those roles for *other* people, but I have nobody in my life I can count on. I give and give, but don't have anybody pouring back into my life." We immediately went to work on hiring the right tribe and firing the people who were sucking the life out of her.

One last example is a client who realized she needed to "fire" someone from one role in her tribe and hire them into a different role. This often happens with the dreamer and devil's advocate, as was the case with this client. She realized her boss is a dreamer while she is a devil's advocate. Suddenly her frustration with him and his frustration with her made a lot more sense. Her practicality continually squelched his dreams. His dreamy ideas continually frustrated her strategic mind. Quitting her job wasn't an option, but she needed to figure out a way for them to work more effectively together. (Note: this required a mental and behavioral shift on her part, not an official face-to-face with her boss.)

He didn't work in her tribe as a Devil's Advocate, but he was a fantastic Dreamer. Firing him meant she stopped asking him to critique her ideas because that's not what dreamers do. Conversely, she prepared for meetings with him, knowing that they weren't going to get into the details or think critically about an idea right away. She prepared a valid critique of his big dreams and shared it after a few days when he was less emotionally attached to those new ideas. The result has meant a better working relationship where she appreciates his dreamer approach and he appreciates her Devil's Advocate critiques (with suggestions) a few days later.

Something else I find interesting as I've polled my audiences about this pairing is that Devil's Advocates and Dreamers are often married. Unfortunately, as a result of this pairing, Devil's Advocates often get a bad rap as "dream killers." If you haven't guessed already, I'm a Dreamer, who also happens to be married to a Devil's Advocate. What I have come to appreciate about my Devil's Advocate wife is that her "how is that going to work?" or "I'm not sure that's a good idea because..." challenges are really just examples of her loving me well. Hear me on this. Because I have my head in the clouds with how things *could* be, I'm often (read mostly) oblivious to the pitfalls, cliffs and snares that I am about to stumble into with one of my grand ideas. My wife, and I believe most Devil's Advocates, love their dreamers so much that they don't want to see them fail. Their natural instinct is to point out the reasons something won't work. They are not killing our dreams even though it feels like it. They are merely proving how much they truly love us. It took me awhile, but when I finally grasped this truth, a stunning change took place in my life and in our marriage.

Okay. Enough examples. Let's dive into the three stages of a Tribal Inventory.

Admire

There is a great Ted Talk called *Everyday Leadership* by Drew Dudley.[6] Google his name or the title and you'll easily find it. Well worth the six-minute investment. In it, Dudley talks about what he calls lollipop moments—moments that other people have shared with us that have made a profound impact. They become an integral part of our stories. He goes further to say that we walk around with this memory of an experience of major significance, we may even tell the story to others, but we've never taken the time to tell the person who was the catalyst for that experience and how they changed us.

I find the same is often true in our tribes. Those people you trust with your deepest secrets, with your kids, with your earthly possessions, with that phone call in the wee hours of the night— these are your tribe members. Some know it. Several don't. And why not? That is what Dudley asks his viewers. Why don't we take the time to let these people know how much they mean to us? So now's the time. Send a text, write a letter, make a call. Be intentional about admiring those you can't imagine life without. Lollipop licked.

Hire

Now that you've completed the admire stage of your Tribal Inventory, you may realize you are lacking some key members. How do you find these people if you don't have them? Hello! Unless you are a hermit, (and maybe especially if you are) the best advice I can give you is look around. Neighborhood, work, church, LinkedIn, Facebook, parent group, gym. I have asked people that I meet, current friends and "suggested connections" on LinkedIn to be members of my tribe. I'm constantly looking to add new members who possess skills and expertise that I lack. Sometimes it's as simple as a message via social media asking them to join and briefly describing why I'd like them to join my tribe and the role they can fill. The right ones will say yes. Most are flattered you asked. The ones that say no, those aren't the ones you need anyway. Don't take it personally. It's amazing what happens when you ask. Focus on the ones that say yes. Crackle, pop. Crackle, pop.

Fire

You may have people in your tribe that somehow always manage to hold you back. Maybe it's their pride. Maybe they struggle with jealousy or arrogance. Maybe their own insecurities drive them to negative behavior. Whatever it is, it can be toxic. You may have people that you have continually gone to for support only to be bludgeoned by questions and criticism. These people could be your parents, friends, co-workers, or maybe even your spouse. As you think about your interactions with these tribe members and the key descriptors of each, ask yourself if they are in the right role in your tribe. If not, they may need to be fired from one role and hired into another, just like in the case of the Devil's Advocate and Dreamer. As you work through your tribal inventory, there may even be some circumstances where people need to be fired from your tribe altogether. I'm not saying you cut these people out of your life completely, but rather look at how they love and support you. Or how they don't. If they aren't what you need, then you have a difficult decision to make. Sometimes this will require a tough conversation to let this person know you can't be around them any longer. Other times this may simply be a choice not to call or otherwise engage someone who has historically been critical and unsupportive of you.

Here's a question I hear a lot when I discuss firing someone in your tribe: "How do I fire my mother!?!?" (That may be the subject of my next book!)

If you start with admiring those already in your tribe and hiring those you lack, the firing stage might not be as difficult as you think. Regardless of the order you use, it is paramount that you take some time for a tribal inventory and then set a plan in motion for action. Listen, don't ignore this. Surrounding yourself with the right people is powerful!

In his book, *Tribe*, Seth Godin challenges, "When you are leading a tribe, a tribe that you belong to, the benefits increase, the work gets easier, and the results are more obvious. That's the best reason to overcome the fear."[7] Fear is real, and often paralyzes; however, paralysis doesn't need to be our final destination. I'm living out this reality while writing this book. The WhatIfAbouts have waged a bitter assault on my courage and tenacity, and fear has been their most effective weapon. Fear of failing, fear of people laughing, fear of no one caring, fear of feeling fear—all of these threaten me every single day (even as I'm typing these words). Jack Canfield is a writer and motivational speaker that I follow. I've learned much from him and often use his quotes when I speak. One of my favorite quotes of his is, "Everything you want is on the other side of fear."[8] As I blow fresh oxygen on my ember, as I see it start to come to life, courage grows and fear shrinks. Little by little I'm seeing what Canfield talks about. At different times, my tribe coaxes me, carries me, kicks me or cheers me to the other side. The point is they are active and involved and I'm not facing it all by myself. My Fire Starters didn't face it alone either.

Take Brandee of Native Ink. At the beginning, her tribe was her mom, dad and a friend of the family, Bob. Bob was the one who initially helped Brandee stoke the ember enough that it threw off some heat. Art was her passion and she decided to pursue it. As she stoked the ember, the heat increased. Alongside Bob came

Brandee's mom and dad. Mom chipped in money for the apprenticeship that she had been saving for Brandee's graduation present. Mom and Dad sat down with Brandee to calculate how much she would need to start the business. Bob remained involved, but his role had become more of a behind the scenes advocate. When Brandee's fledgling tribe was tapped out (neither mom, dad nor Bob had started a business before), the tribe needed to grow. Enter, the banker. The banker became an adviser—here's what you need to do, here's what I need you to figure out, here's what I need you to come back with. For over twenty-one years Brandee has been creating body art for people in her studio and around the country. Surprisingly, she's still with the same bank! We are loyal to our tribe and they are loyal to us.

What about Runner Girl? Very soon after her phone call from the doctor's office, she got her tribe around her and announced that changes were going to be made. Runner Girl has a "driver" personality. Here's a problem, time to fix it. Make a list--check it off. She had the support of her husband when she announced, "If dinner isn't ready or the house isn't clean, you need to understand I'm taking care of me." She went on to find a group of people that could relate to her struggles and joined Weight Watchers. That support and accountability was just what Runner Girl needed at that time to reach her goal of losing 50 pounds and becoming a lifetime Weight Watchers member. Since losing that initial weight, she has run several organized races including three half marathons!

Along the way, she fired one tribe, Weight Watchers, and hired another. Her new tribe is full of committed wellness and fitness professionals passionate about whole body wellness called Revelation Wellness. (Check them out at revelationwellness.org.) Runner Girl recently completed an intensive training course and is now a certified health and fitness instructor with Revelation Wellness. Her tribe has grown within this organization to include people across the country and around the world. They have

Facebook pages and video chat apps that they use to encourage one another and promote accountability. At one point, four of these women plus Runner Girl met for a week of tribal growth and rest. Some traveled almost all the way across the country to be present for the week. Tribal connections are strong and speak to our deepest heart. We trust them to see "behind the curtain" and not judge, laugh or run away from what they see!

As a continued loyal member of her tribe, Runner Girl's husband attended the same training course and was also certified as an instructor. They are taking their fire to the inner city and working with a youth organization to help kids move intentionally while teaching them about healthy eating and setting good habits at an early age.

220 Leadership experienced a powerful benefit from a connector in their tribe. I'm pleased to say that the connector is yours truly! Joseph and Matthew live in Chicago, but their family and extended network are in Indianapolis where I live. From time to time we get together when they are in town. I love it when this happens, because I walk away from our interactions so energized. Their passion and optimism about their vision and mission are contagious. These conversations push me to constantly re-evaluate my own calling and plan, and inspire me to work harder. The Moheban brothers are the perfect combination of Listener and Dreamer. They ask intentional questions and then listen...and then follow up with more intentional questions and, in the process, inspire me.

It was on one of their trips through Indianapolis as they were headed to a weekend retreat to dream and brainstorm and strategize about where to go with 220 that we met for coffee. As I listened to their plans and goals for their time away I felt compelled to tell them about a member of my tribe that deserves huge gratitude for her part in the words you are currently reading. Jenni Robbins of Ignite Development (www.ignitetoday.com) has worked with some amazing people to hone their message and their framework. In my own personal journey, she has fulfilled several tribal member roles—sometimes multiple roles in one meeting. After coffee and time with the brothers, I sent an email introduction to both parties and recommended they meet. They did and if you were to ask either side, they would each tell you the synergy that has come from working together has been magical. This makes me so happy! 220 is now focused in a way they never have been, and Ignite Development has a new client, a glowing referral, and a chance to work with some amazing pioneers in the world of leadership.

What's even better (from a purely selfish standpoint) is this: Joseph called one day and said he had good news for me. As solid members of my tribe who support me, they had put a link on their website to a local TEDx inspired event where I had spoken. 220 Leadership had done a session at a huge national conference the year before and the brothers' contact had seen my video. She wanted me to come and be one of the keynote speakers and talk about the concept of WhatIfAbouts! Not only had the support of my tribe led to this speaking gig, it validated my content and gave me a large platform to craft and hone that message—all while boosting my confidence that I was on the right path.

This is what happens when you allow your ember to heat up—it grows. Others are attracted to the flame you are tending, and they gather round. This adds fuel to the fire. The fire grows. As more gather, more are invited. More fuel. And on and on. Find your tribe. Plug in. Dig deep. Invest.

Just as Fire Dad busts through doors and searches rooms to find those that are lost in the burning building and pulls them out, so members of our tribe are there to pull us out of the smoke when we need them. They have clear vision when we can't see the door in front of us. While we have been bumping around in the dark, they know the quickest way from point A to B. We need them and saying yes to their area of expertise is key to the success of our flame. After all, isn't that what all this fire-starting business is about?

My family and I love the show *The Voice*, partly because we enjoy music on several levels, and partly because we like to guess who will be chosen and who won't. I'm borderline obsessed with watching it and we often binge watch on Sunday afternoons. I'm not obsessed with who is on what team or who moves on from round to round. I'm obsessed with the process of what happens when people go for their dreams, take a HUGE risk, crush their performance, have others speak new life into their dreams and watch their lives transform. I must admit something else here, too, that only my wife and children know about me when I watch this show. My daughter sums it up best when she looks at me and says, "Dad, are you crying...*again*...?" So, there it is.

In one memorable episode, a woman was struggling with confidence and being herself and (I can't believe I'm about to quote Billy Ray Cyrus here) he said, "Live like there is no box. Be who you are and don't be afraid." It was a watershed moment for this woman, and her performance was quite something to behold—through blurry eyes I might add. Her life was literally transformed by this tribe of people that had surrounded her and breathed new life into her confidence and her dreams. Countless times I've heard the contestants say, "If I could get just one chair to turn, that would prove this is all worth it." "If I could just get one chair to turn, it would convince me that this is what I am made to do." One contestant really rocked me when she said, "I need a chair to turn to believe in myself again."

~You need a tribe, plain and simple~

Please don't miss this point. Our society has made the "lone wolf" thing admirable and mysterious and sexy in some cases, but it's a lie. You *could* do it alone, but why *would* you? Life is hard enough in itself, why add loneliness and doubt and fear to the mix?

My dad is 78 years old and a foundational member of my tribe. He's a classic Dreamer, full of ideas like, 'you could do this' OR 'you could do that' OR 'you could do something else altogether.' He has inspired me and encouraged me to follow my dreams. After I shared *The Voice* story in my weekly Friday Freestyle email, the "live like there is no box" idea seemed to have struck a chord with several people. My dad was one of them. Here's what he wrote to me in an email response: "I've lived most of my life outside the BOX. I'm at the age where reflection on life comes into play pretty regularly. I recently read, 'Be who you are because everybody else is taken.' I might add, do it without fear; do it with conviction and honesty."

I might add the same for you.

Find your tribe.

Love them hard.

Let them love you back.

Let them in, especially into the scary places.

As you pour out your heart before them like those artists on *The Voice*, I believe in the deepest part of my soul, their support will overwhelm you.

Live like there is no box.

STOP

At this point I'd like to ask you to do something no other author has probably asked of their readers. Stop reading. Seriously. Put the book down and spend a few days in reflection by answering the following questions:

What is your ember? If you don't know, I encourage you to go to www.firestarterstribe.com and explore the options for my "30 Days to Blaze" program.

There are 4 options available. They vary based on the level of support and accountability you want, and are listed under the "Store" tab.

Option 1—*Single Match*—this option is perfect if you are a committed self-starter and want to work at your own pace. Order the workbook, find your fire and fan your flame.

Option 2—*Book of Matches*—this option is designed for a group that wants to take this journey together. Meet every week for 4 weeks and follow the leader guide to maximize your time and fan your individual and collective flames.

Option 3—*Camp Fire*—Led by me, this 4-week online course meets virtually for 75 minutes every week for accountability and tribe building as you find your fire and fan your flame. **Check website for availability.

Option 4—*Fire Side Chat*—you are serious about making major changes and need a personal guide. This option is customized to you and your unique challenges. **Contact Fire Starters Inc. to set up a free, no obligation, 30-minute phone consultation

Who is in your tribe? Spend time filling out your Tribal Inventory to make sure you have the right people surrounding and supporting you.

What is one major fear you've identified while you read? Fear is real. It's important to start recognizing your WhatIfAbouts so you can beat them back and eventually overcome them. Consider using the **DOing** page to start working on those WhatIfAbouts.

The **DOing** Page

Take some time to reflect and jot down 1-3 reactions you have to what you just read and make sure one is active that you will **DO!**

Extra **DOing** space in case you need it.

EXTINGUISHERS

A grandfather took his son to visit the gravesite of his recently deceased grandmother. They talked of life and death and the afterlife and how this woman had impacted both of their lives. In listening to his grandfather, he learned some things he never knew about her. She was brave and courageous and was a catalyst for change in her community.

As they were walking back to the car, the boy took his grandfather's hand, looked up into his eyes and thanked him for sharing those stories about his grandmother. He confessed that there were many things he didn't know about her and how inspired he was now that he had learned more about her life. At that, his grandfather stopped, took the boy by the shoulders and gently turned him around to face the vast cemetery before them. They stood there quiet for a time until finally his grandfather broke the silence.

"Grandson, look at all of those head stones. Each one represents a life and a story—an amazing story. Think how many of those stories will never be told and never be heard. Live your life out loud so that it tells your story."

This is a challenge to all of us. What are you doing to tell your story, to leave your legacy, to fan your flame? You see that need, you feel that void and you purpose to move forward and make a difference. You stoke that ember and smoke and heat start to emanate. It's working. The fire is starting to catch. Excitement builds. You can almost feel the warmth and see the flame and then. . .

WHOOSH!

When you look around your day-to-day world you will see many tools that have been designed to extinguish fires. All extinguishers have one common purpose—kill the flame! These exist in the buildings we visit and homes we live in as smoke detectors, sprinkler systems, fire extinguishers, fire hoses, fire hydrants. There are even whole firefighting companies (like Fire Dad's) living in fire houses ready to respond at a moment's notice and put out the fire.

In all my interviews with the Fire Starters, such extinguishers existed. No exception. They came in different forms with different faces, but they were ever present.

In writing this book, I searched for the perfect word to describe these extinguishers. Some people use the acronym ANTS (Automatic Negative Thoughts). Head trash is another popular term. After searching dictionaries and thesauruses, I decided I'd make up my own word. I've taught English around the world for the better part of twenty years. You may disagree, but I think this experience gives me the right to make up my own word for these extinguishers, so I did!

WhatIfAbouts. You know them. They are as familiar as your best friend growing up. And they are as automatic as swallowing when you take a drink. They sound something like this.

You: Hey I see a need here. I should do X.

WhatIfAbout: That'll never work. Too hard. Terrible idea.

You: But nobody else is doing X and lots of people need it.

WhatIfAbout: Nope, nope, nope. That's crazy. It'll never work.

You: I think it could work. If I do this and that and put that together...

WhatIfAbout: What makes you so smart? What have you ever done that qualifies you to be the one? You're not listening. IT WILL NEVER WORK!!

You: Ehh, that'll probably never work.

I could recreate this scenario again and again with business ideas, service ideas, parenting ideas, weight loss and fitness ideas, relationship ideas, management ideas. . . I could dial up or dial down the WhatIfAbouts attack on your character, lack of resources, lack of support and/or the stupidity of your idea, but the end result (mostly) ends up the same. The WhatIfAbouts win. Even as the idea is spawning, it's under attack by the WhatIfAbouts. If successful, their attack moves us quickly from the excitement phase of that new idea to dejection and dismissal.

It happens so quickly, that most of us don't even realize it. We move through the process like our daily commute. We suddenly find ourselves at our destination with no real awareness or recollection of how we got there.

If we want to keep peeling back the onion on the WhatIfAbouts, we could start by listing them as fears. Shall we?

I can't do X because I'm afraid of:

Looking stupid

Trying

*Failing. . .**again***

The unknown

What others will say

Losing money

Damaging my reputation

So, there's a start. If that list doesn't cover it for you, here's some space to include your own. Go ahead. Write it down. Put it in the light. A mentor of mine used an acronym for this very process. PTTOTT—Put the Turd On the Table. A bit crass? Yep. Appropriate? You betcha.

This is your opportunity to put a name on the WhatIfAbout that snuffs out your ember.

What did you write down?

For some of you, it is painfully obvious and writing it down is easy, but it hurts. Some of you may be encountering this fire hose face-to-face for the first time. If that's the case, take some time to dig in to your WhatIfAbout and ask yourself some questions.

1. Where does it come from?
2. Do you see its effects in other areas?
3. Is it legitimate? How?
4. If you answered yes to #3, spend some time answering why.

Now that we've given this thing a name, it's necessary to take the next step and ask one very simple question.

Ready?

Here it is...

So what?!

Seriously? Seriously.

Now that this thing has a name, take a good hard look at it and ask, "So what?!" Remember, you've got to go through the fear to get to the other side. Consider one major WhatIfAbout in your life. What's on the other side of it? How are you going to get there? Don't just let this be a question you ponder. Use it to fuel specific action.

I did.

It was my first keynote for "real money "and I had big plans. The entire audience would get up and play Rock, Paper Scissors to prove one of my points; I would show a funny clip from the TV show *Friends*; and I would get someone from the audience to light something on fire.

Before letting you know how it all went down, I want to give you a look behind the curtain of my WhatIfAbouts. They were on full attack mode.

These people are adults, there's no way they'll play Rock, Paper, Scissors with you. That's a dumb idea.

Technology won't work. What's going to happen then, huh? Everyone will laugh, and your presentation will be a failure.

You're a failure.

They're paying you HOW MUCH? Are you kidding me? You're not worth it!

Who are you to speak to anyone on any topic? You're an imposter and they'll see that as soon as you step on stage.

You're going to wear those clothes? Really? You look ridiculous.

Nobody in their right mind would volunteer to come on stage and set something on fire. It'll never work.

There were more, but I think you get the picture. We all have these WhatIfAbouts and they are really good at targeting our most insecure places. Even after speaking on stages in front of thousands of people, speaking all over the country and getting paid to do it, my WhatIfAbouts still attack. The difference now is that I've learned to say, with confidence, "So what?!" And let me encourage you with this: Each "so what" showdown with my WhatIfAbouts makes the next one that much easier to win.

So, how did it go? Well, two of three went swimmingly. The Rock, Paper, Scissors worked to get people moving and meet someone new. Let's just say I acted out Joey's part of the *Friends* clip due to video issues... But it was the setting something on fire part that I was most nervous about. The activity challenges each audience member to write down a fear on one side of an index card, while Jack Canfield's quote, "Everything you want is on the other side of fear" is displayed in big letters on the screen. Once they write down the fear I ask them to turn it over and write on the other side of the card what life would look like if that fear were gone.

It was at this point that I asked for a volunteer to come up on stage. It got *really* quiet. The WhatIfAbouts went to work with a vengeance. ***See, nobody is volunteering. This is going to be an epic fail!*** My heart was pounding as I searched the eyes of the audience for a willing volunteer. Finally, I saw a hand go up and invited Brea on stage.

Ha HA! Take **that** WhatIfAbouts!

Now for the setting-on-fire part. I forgot to mention a key detail. This conference was being held at the Indiana Historical Society, and the room we occupied was entirely walled with wood. How do you spell matchbox? If I wanted this to go as planned, it was clearly a time to ask for forgiveness later instead of permission in advance.

I'm not an idiot! I obtained a metal mixing bowl full of water from the kitchen and needed a volunteer to hold it. I even got a kitchen worker to loan me his lighter... Once this was all set I gave Brea the lighter while I held her index card and she set it on fire. If you want to see a picture of this in action, go to www.firestarters.com and choose the "Hire Jason" option under the "Contact" tab. What a fire starter moment! Literally. I invite you to create a similar fire starter moment for yourself. This exercise is powerful for many reasons:

1. It gets the fear out of your head and down on paper so you can see it. Now it's manageable.
2. Turning the paper over and writing what is on the other side of fear gives you permission to go beyond the fear and run your mind through positive scenarios instead of staying stuck in the WhatIfAbout.
3. Setting fire to the paper is both a torching of your fear and an igniting of your dream.
4. It is a small but powerful **ACTION** step in overcoming your WhatIfAbout.

One more exercise I recommend when dealing with fears is to set a timer when you start to feel stressed and your mind starts spinning with the "What about this?" and "What if that?" questions. Allow yourself 5 or 10 minutes to think about what could go wrong. For me as a dreamer, this is especially important. I tend to avoid the negative side of things at all costs. Setting this timer allows you to give time and space to think about the pitfalls and reasons something may not work. When the timer goes off, reset it for the same number of minutes and use this time to consider all the positive things that could happen. Give equal time to both sides of the equation instead of just letting fear hog all the time.

Retelling this story and its accompanying WhatIfAbouts has been good review for me. I am powerfully reminded that my WhatIfAbouts don't define me. It's proof that saying "so what?" to them really works. It will also work for you. And it also works for my Fire Starters.

As I interviewed all the Fire Starters for this book, **ALL** of them used this strategy. They looked at their WhatIfAbouts with intention and legitimately asked, "So *what*?!" It helped that they had answers. Check out what they had to say.

<u>Native Ink</u>—*How am I going to do this? Nobody in my family has ever started a business before...*
- *So what if I fail?* I'd rather fail trying than not try at all.
- *So what if I'm only 18 and a girl and have no idea how to start a business...*I've learned what customers want and need and I know I can provide them with that service.
- *So what if this doesn't work?* I have had other jobs. I can find another job.

Now an accomplished tattoo artist of NFL and NBA players, musicians and thousands of other satisfied clients around the country.

<u>Runner Girl</u>—How am I going to get healthy with everything else I have going on with kids, the house and my husband?
- *So what if I've never exercised before and don't know what I'm doing?* I have some workout DVDs that start simple and

move to more advanced stages that I can follow in the comfort of my own home.

- *So what if I've never run any significant distance?* I found a "couch to 5K" running plan for free online that takes a systematic approach and is easy to follow.
- *So what if things around the house aren't perfect while I focus on getting healthy?* I can handle things not being "just the way I want them" in exchange for better health. I'll also ask my husband and kids to pitch in more and support me.

Now a certified fitness and wellness instructor with Revelation Wellness and certified Holy Yoga instructor.

Fire Dad—A veteran fire fighter of seventeen years working many hours and extra shifts to support his family. He wanted more quality time with the ones he loved the most. He felt a responsibility to lead his family well, and in doing so teach them to deal with and overcome failure.

- *So what if I failed in the past?* I may fail again, but that fear is not going to keep me from trying.
- *I'm not sure I'm doing this right.* I will rely on my wife as my partner through this and we will lean on each other and our faith. We'll make mistakes and we'll learn from them.

Now Homeschooler, supportive husband of 18+ years and father of four; middle school youth leader. AND a firefighter.

220 Leadership--Both found themselves in corporate jobs going through the motions and trying to climb the corporate ladder while feeling unfulfilled and stuck.

- *So what if we walk away from promising corporate careers?* We may be making money, but we're not living out our purpose.
- *So what if our friends and family think we're crazy?* This isn't the first crazy idea we've had.
- *So what if money gets tight?* We can drive Uber and dip into our savings if we need to.

Well, they did drive for Uber and tap their savings.

Now, run workshops around the country and make money to support themselves and the business.

The Fire Starters cared more about trying and failing than not trying at all. Sound familiar? If you see yourself reflected in these words, and you're still waiting for 'everything to be in order,' you need to stop waiting. It's time for action. It's your turn. That last thought is worth repeating. It's. Your. Turn. Are you listening?

In addition to having answers to their "So what?!", these Fire Starters had another thing in common. After getting them to list their WhatIfAbouts for me in our interviews, I asked them how many of them came true. More or less the answer was something like, "None of them, really."

Wait! What? Mic check! Yep. That's right.

~None of them, really. . .~

Does this mean people didn't think they were crazy? No, a few did— maybe. Did this mean that the unknown wasn't scary? No, it was— sometimes very much so. BUT NOT NEARLY AS SCARY AS THEY THOUGHT IT WAS GOING TO BE!

Are you still with me? Are you soaking this in?

Getting down on your hands and knees and breathing life into your ember is no guarantee that it will suddenly burst into flame. All of these Fire Starters emphasized the hard work of stoking their embers into flames. That admission was followed almost immediately by a statement like, "<u>BUT</u>, when you're doing what you love, it doesn't really feel like work."

~When you're doing what you love, it doesn't really feel like work~

Here they come! Right on cue. Those pesky WhatifAbouts... They are relentless! In fact, yours might just be listed below.

But my idea couldn't succeed like theirs did.

I don't have enough time, skill, money, education.

I don't even know where to start.

Did you see them coming this time? You will. Trust me. The more you stand up to them and ask, "So what?", the easier it is to stoke the ember into a flame instead of letting the WhatifAbouts suck out the air and extinguish the flame. They become more obvious over time, and the more you stand up to them, the more you realize they are mostly paper dragons. And guess what gets rid of paper dragons best and quickest?

Yes! FIRE!

I knew you were with me.

As powerful and effective as fire is, we are conditioned from an early age that we shouldn't touch it or go near it. **Don't play with fire. You'll get burned!** Most every kid in America and around the world has heard this dire warning. It comes from a scolding adult wagging a finger in our faces for our own good. While on a short getaway with my wife, I heard a grandfather yell this to his three grandsons who were amusing themselves with an outdoor torch. Father Bear was hot on the heels of Grandpa's warning and took it to the next level with a mini lecture off to the side for the oldest boy—no doubt telling him he should know better and should also be thinking about the example that he's setting for his younger brothers.

As a father myself, I have trumpeted similar warnings. They are necessary to 6 and 10-year-old boys ready to torch a match house built on a wooden kitchen table while alone downstairs. . .

These same types of warnings are echoed throughout our lifetime by parents, teachers, friends, boyfriends, girlfriends, wives and husbands, co-workers and even casual observers. Good will is in ample supply when these warnings are offered. The problem is that these well-meaning cautioners most often speak those warnings from their own place of fear or inexperience. They no doubt have a quick example they can pull up from someone's daughter that had a friend who tried the same thing and, well, "we all know what happened to her. . ." Most assuredly they have our best interest at heart and I'm convinced they genuinely believe they are helping us along the way. Their warning is keeping us from an unavoidable pitfall that our youth, lack of experience, lack of time, lack of money, lack of organizational skills, lack of *something* will surely lead us into.

I don't begrudge them the warning, but I do begrudge them the effect it has on us. They act as fire extinguishers or fire hoses being emptied out on a nearly suffocated ember. Sometimes the warning charges in like a whole fire brigade attacking a flame with the full force of the firehouse, eager to stamp out any hint of heat or flame.

If you've ever been told to "be careful so you don't get burned," you can relate. You've had an ember that sparked up and created a bit of heat and got you moving. It goes like this. Your mind starts going a thousand miles an hour, your pulse quickens, you may even get out some paper and start brainstorming. You write down a few things, let a few daring thoughts loose, and begin to dream. Quick on the heels of that process comes a regrettable visit by the WhatIfAbouts to douse the smoldering ember. You try desperately to stay on your hands and knees and blow life into this thing and then, WHOOSH! That well-meaning extinguisher empties her bucket, smothering the flame just as it began to really burn. Smoke and ash billow out and you are left with nothing but soot on your face and cold ashes where, just moments before, spark and energy and heat had been. Not a good time to be alone, because at precisely this moment, the WhatIfAbouts swoop back in with a chorus of "I told you so!" and "What were you thinking?"

How do you get the fire started again? How do you muster up the strength to dig the ember out of the ash, blow life into it and fan it into a flame? Some might. Most won't--especially if they are alone. You must rely on your tribe. They pull you up, dust you off and blow life into you so you can do the same for your ember. Fire Starting is hard work and you need your tribe. Those extinguishers? They don't stop.

Since I began writing this book, I've gathered plenty of evidence to prove that point. One that struck a chord with me features the recording superstar, Adele. Regardless of how you feel about her music, you cannot deny the success and popular appeal it has had all over the world. Consider this excerpt from a 2015 interview on NPR the first week that her album *25* was released. "Her latest LP, *25,* has sold more copies than any other album in its first week of release — more than 2.4 million so far — and the week is only half over. Its first single, "Hello," has been the No. 1 song on the *Billboard* Hot 100 chart since it came out four weeks ago. It's quaint to think that, before *25* was launched upon an adoring public, *Adele was expressing concern that her fans might have forgotten about her* in the nearly five years since *21,* a record-breaker in its own right."[9]

Are you paying attention? *Half way* through the FIRST week of her new album's release it was already the number 1 selling album of all time for that time frame. "Hello" wound up staying at the top of the charts for 10 weeks—almost 2 ½ months! Her album *21* was a huge smash, she traveled the world, made piles of money and..." was expressing concern that her fans might have forgotten about her." What?

Indulge me one more musical example. In 2016, our oldest son introduced my wife and me to the band, *Twenty One Pilots*. It's two guys—one sings and plays the instruments—piano, guitar, ukulele to name a few, and the other plays drums. They do some weird stuff on stage with masks. They're a little 'out there' in some ways, but I really enjoy their music and their lyrics. Apparently, I'm not alone. At the time of this writing, their number one song on Spotify has 951 million listens and the next two have a combined 1.5 billion listens. (Undoubtedly those numbers will be higher by the time you are reading this.) On those three songs, they have over 2.5 BILLION listens with almost 14 million monthly listeners—and this is just on Spotify. Let that soak in for a minute.

When we saw them in concert in 2016, the lead singer climbed up a scaffold—spot light shining on him and music looping in the background—and said (and I'm paraphrasing here): We want to thank our parents who are in the audience for believing in us and encouraging us to pursue our dreams because we are living our dream in this moment, here with all of you. When we started out we didn't tell anybody about our dream because we were afraid they would laugh, but here we are. Thanks to all of you for believing in us and allowing us a chance to live our dream.

~When we started out we didn't tell anybody...

we were afraid they would laugh...~

But they did it. And guess what? People responded. Not with laughing either. In 2017 they were nominated for three Grammy Awards and won the Grammy for Best Pop Duo/Group Performance. They accepted the Grammy in their boxers. There's a whole story that goes with that and you should look up the video clip. Google "Twenty One Pilots Grammy" and you'll find it. Notably, lead singer Tyler said as he held up the Grammy, "Anyone from anywhere can do anything and this is that."

As I sit here reflecting on this story and Adele's story and other notable figures in history who have led or pioneered in some way and their stories, I'm struck. Struck by the wild anticipation, the sheer possibility of WHAT IF? This is not a WhatIfAbout, but a moment of wondering. What if???

What if Van Gogh, Rembrandt, Dali or Monet had never painted?

What if Bono, Dylan, Joplin, Hendrix, Cash had never made music?

What if John Maxwell, Seth Godin or Brene Brown thought they didn't have anything to say?

The list is long, and so is the impact these and so many others have had on their tribes, their communities and the world. I wonder how many of them ever thought their reach and impact would be so vast? I doubt many did. I think they were doing what they loved, and it set their souls on fire in the best possible way. Maybe they hoped that their impact and legacy would be great. I don't know. What I do know is that the anthems of my life would be very different without U2 songs in the world and my love of all things Tribe and desire to start and share something like this book may never have happened without the influence of Seth Godin's writing.

Here's another "what if" that I'm learning to dare out of me. What if I could be someone's Seth Godin and make a lasting impact on others like he did on me? Talk about challenging the WhatIfAbouts! I say that and it's like I'm squaring off in a Roman coliseum with these WhatIfAbout beasts. Here's what it sounds like in my head:

WIA: You? Like Seth Godin? Insert the sound of mocking laughter.

Me: Well some guy who gets published in Inc. Magazine on a regular basis told me he liked my tribe stuff better than Seth's and that really surprised me and made me feel good about what I'm doing.

WIA: (more mocking laughter) Who is he? He's one person and most people don't even know him. His opinion doesn't matter. Also, who do you think you are? You're a fake and a fraud.

Me: But I get emails from people that tell me that I inspire them or make them think or challenge them. They tell me to keep doing what I'm doing because I've made a difference.

These are merely a snippet of the WhatIfAbouts that daily try to trip me up as I chase my dream. Some days it's more intense than others. Some days I'm strong and some days I just don't want to fight. People often think that when they see someone on the "big stage," or when they've reached a certain level of success that the WhatIfAbouts disappear. Not true. They simply change their tactics and approach. They're still present. They still pester. A member of my tribal council said something to me recently that is applicable here. We were talking about doubts and fears and WhatIfAbouts and she said, "When I start to battle with self-doubt, shame, guilt or whatever is after me that day, I ask myself if this is a 'BIG T truth' or just a belief." She went on to explain that she deliberately slows down and takes a quick inventory of wins, remembers what her tribe has told her, and re-focuses on what she knows her ember is. She gathers up that positive energy and true evidence and stacks it all against the negative belief(s) threatening her. More often than not, she's successful in extinguishing the WhatIfAbouts. That's a good exercise for us all.

For two solid years, the WhatIfAbouts kept me scared and stuck. Looking back on those two years now, I'm pissed that I listened to them for as long as I did and *so* wish I had known about that exercise. At the same time, I'm aware that these struggles I endured and my battles with my WhatIfAbouts are what have made me who I am today. It's all necessary—the realization of my OD, the prodding of my tribe and the willingness to take one (sometimes *extremely* small) step forward were all necessary as I committed myself to building my fire. My fire is not the same as yours. Your fire is different from the Fire Starters in this book. But all of our fires share the common ground of hard work and dedication, as you'll see in the next chapter.

The **DOing** Page

Take some time to reflect and jot down 1-3 reactions you have to what you just read and make sure one is active that you will **DO!**

Extra **DOing** space in case you need it.

FLAME

Prepare the ground. Collect the wood. Stack it just so. Strike the match. Fan the flame. All of this is part of the hard and often tedious work of building the fire. This is what my Fire Starters committed to. It's also what I've committed to as I've taken the leap to be on my own. It's what you must commit to if you are to enjoy the warmth and crackle of the flame of your ember. Check out these inside looks at the building process for my fire and for those of my Fire Starters.

After putting a framework around her dream, Brandee had to meet her WhatIfAbouts head-on. Every doubt she encountered she responded with, "So what?!" (Just a reminder that you'll have to do this too.)

The next step required action.

Brandee went to a local bank and shared her story and her passion about opening a tattoo shop that focused on extraordinary customer service. The banker recommended calculating her startup costs. She and her parents made the list. It totaled $3,000. With of host of butterflies in her stomach, she met with the banker and...

The banker laughed her out of the bank, told Brandee she was a foolish girl with a crazy pipe dream and that the bank would never fund such an absurd business venture!

NO!

Actually, just the opposite happened. The bank gave her a personal loan for $3000 and Native Ink was launched! Twenty-one years later, she's still with that same bank.

Next step? Find a place to set up shop. Brandee's sister-in-law just happened to have a hair salon with some extra, unused space. She offered it to Brandee. Two of three challenges conquered. Tiny flames began to dance.

Startup capital? Check. Space? Check. Now to conquer #3—finding customers. These days, Brandee recognizes that if she'd had the immediate exposure of social media, getting the word out about

Native Ink would have been so much easier. Instead, "I hung flyers within a twenty-mile radius of my shop. I hung them anywhere and everywhere—bulletin boards, grocery stores, light poles at busy intersection." And guess what? The customers started to come. They didn't come in droves and it wasn't an overnight success, but they came.

At this point, Native Ink as Brandee's side hustle. She was still going to school and working at an auto plant to keep her options open. Bottom line, she was tattooing, and her business was growing.

Fast forward eighteen months when a house that she drove by often and really love came up for sale. It *also happened* to be on a main highway with lots of traffic. It *also had* a detached garage she though would be a great space for a studio.

A quick side note—as you begin to #embracethechase of finding your ember, opportunities that you never imagined will present themselves.

She called a realtor to make an appointment. (She wasn't yet twenty years old!) When she told the realtor about her plans for the house, the realtor didn't take her seriously—who was Brandee to be buying a house?!?! *She was just a young girl with silly ideas about a tattoo business.*

Another quick side note—other people sometimes supply the WhatIfAbouts that you'll face. Or, they'll chirp and nag in your own voice. Either way, the WhatIfABouts will be right there as opportunities emerge. Keep building.

So Brandee gave up? Nope. She fired that relator and found one who took her seriously. She lived in that house for more than fifteen years. Her studio was in the garage, there was a spacious are for her clients to park, and a place her girls could come and join her when she worked. They got a chance to see firsthand what Mom did and learned about running a small business. Only recently she's moved her thriving business into her hometown of Elwood, IN, after selling the very house she bought after hiring some WhatIfAbout realtor!

I loved the pride and satisfaction in Brandee's voice as she reflected on this time. She'd be the first one to tell you that it was hard work. She made mistakes along the way, but also learned form those mistakes and uses them to teach her daughters.

Runner Girl's certification as a group fitness instructor didn't come from binge eating and watching Netflix. There were (and still are) early morning workouts, saying no to food and drink that *everyone* around her is devouring, and staying committed to her mission to live and lead others in a whole and healthy life style. That certification process required her to be away from her family for an entire week for an intensive retreat that marked the end of training. There were logistics to work out, money to save for plane tickets and a host of other challenges that were part of this building process. The building has continued for Runner Girl. She has since uncovered more of her ember and has made the decision to get a second master's degree (in her 40s mind you) to become a clinical mental health counselor.

The Moheban brothers had their own set of challenges as they worked to build 220 Leadership. They made some hard decisions to walk away from what was considered normal life for young professionals in their circle. They tell it best on their website:

"We were in jobs that paid pretty well, that we could talk ourselves into as 'the right place to be for now.'

But if we were really honest with ourselves, we knew there was more. One of us traveled every single week for a consulting job, which included two plane rides and four hours in a rental car.

The other worked 72-84 hours per week in finance, wishing away workdays, missing personal commitments, and waiting for weekends and vacation days to enjoy life."

Talk to them today, and they don't even resemble the people you just read about. Are they working hard? Absolutely. Are they making the same money? No. Are they continuing to sacrifice to make their dreams come true? You bet. Would they trade this flame they've so carefully tended for the old life above? No way!

When Fire Dad made the decision to spend more time at home and be a more intentional dad, it was hard work. Less money had to be stretched further, but fewer shifts provided more opportunity to be just Dad. As he invested time at home and worked less, there were other opportunities that presented themselves. He was asked to join the church staff where he and his family attend to lead the middle school youth group. So, not only was he spending more time with his kids, he was being paid to invest that time in his kids and other youth as well.

Such an opportunity wasn't even remotely an idea when he took fewer shifts to be intentional at home! Fire Dad #embracedthechase and intentionally worked on building that inner fire. Sacrifices of time and money were necessary and painful at times. This is the work of fire building.

In April of 2017, I registered Fire Starters Inc. as an official business entity. I had hope that it would grow into *something*, but didn't have a clear idea of what that might be. I just knew it was time to take that first real, "official" step. It wasn't as if I hadn't been preparing for this step, though. Quite the contrary.

For the better part of twenty years I had a spiral bound notebook or a manila file folder labeled M.O.B. The contents were not my secret plans for starting an organized crime ring, they were the dreams and ideas for what would one day become My Own Business.

The M.O.B. notebook got its official start in Poland (where I lived for eight years, earned my master's degree and taught at a private university). I would jot down random notes when I didn't have the notebook with me and then shove those between the last page and back cover for safe keeping. Eventually the chaos of the shoved bits of paper and random notes required some organization and I adopted the manila M.O.B folder. We moved back to the U.S. with the plan for me to obtain my Ph.D. and return to Poland or Europe to teach. That was fourteen years ago. I'm clearly still in the U.S. and I did not get back to grad school to start that Ph.D. Turns out it's true, "Life is what happens when we're busy making other plans."

Life happened—and kept happening. We had our daughter (our third child), re-habbed an entire house built in the early 1900s, worked to pay bills and raise kids and put that on repeat. I worked in education because that is what I knew and taught in various adjunct positions while teaching high school full time. I did this for two years, and each of those years, <u>six</u> W-2s from the teaching, restaurant and construction jobs I worked arrived in the mail. I was quickly learning that as much as I loved education, it was hard to make ends meet. I was showing up everywhere but not really being effective anywhere. That's when I discovered the role of corporate trainer.

My initial foray into the corporate world lasted ten years and included jobs in training and development, inside sales, directing inside sales, sales development as a field VP and working on a huge transformation project with mergers and acquisitions as part of an HR team. All the while, I kept adding to the M.O.B. folder. Who do I want my clients to be? What kinds of services do I want to offer? What core values will I build my company's foundation upon? What do I want my brand to stand for? These were the questions I was asking and answering with articles I'd save and dreams and ideas I'd have—often while sitting in pointless corporate meetings talking about the same things we talked about at the last meeting!

Punching the clock turned to drudgery. I felt my OD slipping away. The day my daughter asked, "Daddy, do you like your job?", I faced the reality that it was time for M.O.B. to stop living in a folder with the promise of "someday."

I hoped that 2018 would finally be the year that Fire Starters Inc., the *side* hustle, would become Fire Starters Inc., my *main* hustle. I imagined how it would happen. I had built and published a website and started spreading the word. I was hired for a keynote that paid "real money" and then hired for a leadership workshop with a large, local, well-known company. Momentum was growing. I just needed to figure out how the PTO from my full-time, corporate gig could be stretched far enough so that I could take days off for the side hustle and still have time for a real vacation with the family. Turned out, the corporate gig took care of that for me.

After a 10-year corporate career, I was informed in a 35-miunte meeting with my boss and another HR VP that my job had been eliminated in an ongoing company restructure. Just like that. After turning in my badge, corporate credit card and company laptop, I learned the terms of my severance and was escorted to the exit. It's a surreal feeling to suddenly be standing outside a door you could access anytime you pleased and realize you now need an invitation and an escort to walk through that same door. Over the next few weeks I had a recurring feeling that I'd been thrown off a ship I thought I'd been helping steer, into a life boat that was partially inflated at best. I kept waiting for someone on the ship to look over and check on me while at the same time realizing the boat had already sailed on without the slightest regard for how I was doing.

I did have some co-workers reach out individually, but I'm speaking here of the "corporate ship." I got no messages from the CEO or my boss's boss, who were ultimately responsible for eliminating my job. I'm not sure what I expected, but after ten years, *something* would have been nice.

Let me tell you that, though this may look like a disaster from the outside, it was, in fact, a tremendous relief. Thankfully, a few years prior I'd had an epiphany. I realized that I had become more concerned with the title at the bottom of my business card, and more obsessed with the tribe I needed to break into, than the person I was becoming as I chased after that next title and promotion. I was painfully aware that what I was chasing was not who I truly wanted to be.

At this point, I think M.O.B. really began to take shape. I wrote vision and mission statements for Fire Starters Inc. when I built my website.

Vision: Fight "STUCKEDNESS" by sparking **A-HA!** moments that ignite sustainable change in behavior and culture—especially when daring the status quo.

Mission: "To creatively deliver platform, group and individual sessions designed to challenge and ultimately disrupt established norms and spark lasting change."

The switch really got flipped when I finally realized that my OD was centered in this mission. Compared to my corporate day job's vision and mission, M.O.B. won in a landslide. Literally. NO contest. Fire Starters Inc., with its vision and mission, is my ember. No doubt about it. In fact, much of my vision and mission were crafted in response to those I rode the elevator with every day. Those whose rote responses to "How's it going?" were "Not bad for a Monday," or the tongue-in-cheek "Living the dream!" The level of enthusiasm was the same with both—almost non-existent.

Let me say this, I do not begrudge the day job corporation its decision to let me go. The severance that I received made it possible to pursue more gigs for Fire Starters Inc. while ensuring I had money to keep the roof over my family's heads and pay the bills. I also made a conscious decision to not complain about what did or didn't happen; about what should or shouldn't have happened; about the people who didn't lose their jobs while I did, or how the entire situation was unfair or how I didn't deserve it. NO... I closed that door after walking out of it and believe I have been better for it.

It's common to ask someone you meet for the first time what they do for a living. Just as common is how much of our identity is wrapped up in the title on our business cards along with a description of our daily corporate duties when we answer the question. The 9-5 grind, the morning and afternoon commutes, the endless string of meetings—all become routine... all become not only what we do, but who we are. The routine of stuckedness and the comfort that routine provides take hold.

All too often I hear people dreaming about "someday." When "someday" gets here, *then* I'll take the risk, *then* I'll follow my heart, *then* I'll chase my dream. Hear me. Someday isn't delivered as a nicely wrapped package via UPS. It's not in your next promotion. It's not in the empty nest. It's not in retirement. You cannot find it in your phone. It's in your heart. Don't find yourself on the doorstep of 'someday' realizing that it's nearly here and lamenting, "I guess I'm going to have to get a life sometime soon."

This is a terrible place to be. I believe whoever feels this way still has an ember—that Original Design I've talked about. It's probably buried deep under the ash of broken dreams, broken promises and broken relationships—but it's there. Waiting. What are you going to do?

It should be apparent how much work it takes to build a flame that sustains. And yet, early mornings, selling possessions, fewer shifts at work, walking away from good-paying jobs, hanging flyers on countless telephone poles, and using PTO for the side hustle (just to name a few), these are the commitments Fire Starters are willing to make. "Fire Starter" is not a title everyone earns. And every single one of them deserve recognition. Not, 'everyone gets a trophy' recognition. Nope. Fire building recognition. Sustaining flame recognition. Going against the "that's just the way life is" recognition. But don't miss this. Every Fire Starter I interviewed for this book underscored how much work it took and how hard it was in the process. But NOT ONE of them said it wasn't worth it. Not one of them said they wouldn't do it all over again. I would echo those same answers in my fire building process. Why?

Flame. Creating something that attracts others and serves a deep purpose is invigorating and exhilarating. There's a soul satisfaction that isn't available from the daily grind.

As an ember truly ignites, everything around it heats up. Energy. Light. Warmth. FLAME. The hard work of preparing the ground, stacking the wood just right, blowing fresh air to coax the ember into flame—all of it has come together for the magical moment when the fire starts to dance. There it is. You can see it starting to grow. All that building and huffing and puffing and persevering has ignited the flame, and it is starting to dance gloriously right before your very eyes.

If you've ever walked up to a fire and stuck your hands out or turned your backside to the flame, you have felt that immediate rush of heat wash over your body. You curl toward it like a cat. It feels good. For those first few moments, you let the warmth pour over you like a hot shower. There's a renewal of energy. You feel different when you are close to the flame. Don't you?

Do you know what else? People are drawn to it. Fire becomes a destination point that others are attracted to. They come with expectancy, arms stretched out to catch the heat, and they want to bring others with them to share in the experience. Fire is fascinating and mesmerizing. Fire offers life-giving warmth and dream-building possibility.

One of my favorite memories of growing up is Christmas morning *after* all the presents were opened. There was always a pile of wrapping paper and packaging left in the living room. The smell of coffee and bacon and coffeecake hung thick in the air. As the oldest, I got to start the fire in the fireplace and burn up all the wrapping paper. I took my sweet time watching individual pieces of paper slowly ignite and then burst into flame. When all the paper was burned up, I got to make the fire that would accompany our Christmas morning feast.

The warmth of the dancing flames charmed me. This whole scene was punctuated every couple of seconds by the crackle, pop and snap of the dry wood being consumed. Man, I still love this today. When we camp, I can sit for hours around a flame and watch it dance and listen to it crackle. It's this part of being a Fire Starter, to me, that is most soul-satisfying. I've prepared the ground, I've blown into the ember, I've stoked the coal, I've blown in more fresh oxygen, I've rearranged the wood, I've stoked some more, I've done the work, and finally. . .flame and crackle!

It's at this moment that I can sit back and regain a bit of perspective. I've been so focused on getting this fire going, that I've forgotten about the sun setting, the birds singing, the coffee brewing and, most importantly, all those s'more ingredients waiting to be combined on a melty bed of marshmallow. Mmmm...

~The crackle is where you get to enjoy

the fire that you've started~

You get to put your feet up and stare into the flame and get lost in what you've built. You've worked hard to get here and there is great satisfaction in this moment.

I hope you are seeing some themes emerge from this stage of being a Fire Starter. There is hard work that **must** be realized. No success -- the crackle that proves the fire is burning -- comes easily. The Fire Starters you've learned about are all in various stages. Native Ink is enjoying a multi-year career doing what she loves and, via social media, can share it with the world while simultaneously attracting more customers. Runner Girl is a couple years in -- she's discovered her passion, made a commitment to it, and desires to use it to help others. 220 Leadership took a huge risk when they both walked away from good-paying jobs to pour into their mission and vision full time. As word is spreading, more opportunities are coming their way to speak and engage people in important development discussions. Fire Dad is well established in part-time ministry, fanning that flame but still fighting destructive fires and saving people. You may just be beginning to discover your ember. Stick with it. With some hard work and careful tending, it will continue to grow.

The **DOing** Page

Take some time to reflect and jot down 1-3 reactions you have to what you just read and make sure one is active that you will **DO!**

Extra **DOing** space in case you need it.

M.O.B.

My Own Business is simply "you do you."

What sets your heart on fire? Hopefully you are closer to answering that question now than when you started reading this book. Don't be alarmed if some smoke gets in your eyes. Don't worry if your ember needs more kindling. Keep tending

I've already told you about the notebook and manila folder that housed M.O.B. for so many years. But I also want to share some challenges and pivotal moments in my life that might inspire and motivate you to take action. Here's a partial list.

- C+ in Public Speaking class at Indiana University
- Academic probation freshmen year at Indiana University
- Cumulative undergrad 2.9 GPA
- 2-year stint as a "professional ski bum" in Summit County, Colorado
- Moved to Poland and didn't know how to speak Polish
- Owned and operated a failed coffee shop in Poland
- Earned MA in TEFL with 3.975 GPA
- Successful 5-year teaching career at a Polish university
- Designed and taught a leadership elective
- Rehabbed an old house from roof to basement
- Worked two years in various full and part-time jobs to support my family—with six W-2s both years
- 7 different positions in ten-year corporate career—the last 3 being jobs I helped create
- Started Fire Starters Inc. in 2017 as a side hustle
- Now Chief Fire Starter and Tribe Leader of Fire Starters Inc.
- Hired as a national key note speaker
- Frequent podcast guest

Maybe you see shades of yourself in this list—not great at something the first go 'round, but better the second time. Maybe you did something of significance "a long time ago" but wouldn't know where to start today. Whatever the case, we all have a list to go along with our story. Mine is not special in any way. What is unique about it, however, is that I've made a conscious decision to own it with all of its victories and failures.

This Original Design thing isn't easy. That list includes some seriously hard work. To be honest, though, some of it was also not so hard. Every bit of it built and shaped me, and none of it was by accident. I fell down and I got back up. I made mistakes (some several times) and I learned from them. But I never settled, and I never quit.

I encourage you to take a similar inventory of your life—wins and losses, good times and bad—and see what themes emerge. For me, it was the desire to see **A-HA!** moments spark and come to life in myself and others. My inventory also includes giving a speech for school president in the eighth grade and then again, my junior year of high school and one more time for VP of my fraternity. I won **all** of those competitions. **Despite** that C+ in Public Speaking. I love to speak, and I'm good at it. I got a C+ because I didn't follow the rubric and tried to do it my own way. (So much for that.)

If you're someone who has always been told to get in line, or if you're always asking for forgiveness instead of permission, you're probably more suited to lead than to follow. But no one can follow you if you are not willing to lead.

This was impressed on me a few years ago when I attended the Global Leadership Summit and heard T.D. Jakes speak. He asked two questions that I think about on a weekly and sometimes daily basis. Those questions challenged me then and they challenge me now. I hope they have the same effect on you. Here they are:

Do you have a magnificent vision?

If you are a leader, whose permission are you waiting for to lead?

It just so happened that this conference took place just when my ember had really started to smoke and heat up. The perfect fire triangle had been created and I was primed for combustion. That first question hit me hard. I had a vision, but was it magnificent? I knew the answer before I got done asking myself the question. My vision was not magnificent. There was nothing daring in it—nothing to make my heart race or hands sweat. No magnificence here.

I struggled mightily to answer that second question honestly. I have been a leader for as long as I can remember both in school and at work. I knew this to be a "BIG T truth," yet I was not acting on it. I was waiting for someone at a higher level in the organization to tap me on the shoulder and tell me it was my turn. I was waiting for the "right job" to open up that would give me the promotion or recognition I was hoping and waiting for. Funny thing is, I couldn't have told you what job, exactly, that would be if you'd asked me. It was more of a hope that I would be awarded the "next rung on the ladder." Bottom line? I was not leading myself and certainly wasn't leading anyone else. I was waiting, and in that instance, waiting was a terrible strategy.

In *The 7 Habits of Highly Effective People,* author Stephen R. Covey identifies the concept he calls your "circle of influence"[9]—where you can affect change and have an impact, and your "circle of concern"—where things affect you, but you really don't have any influence or control over circumstances or outcomes. If we aren't careful, we can get stuck in the outer circle of concern where we waste our days away complaining, blaming and waiting for some *else* to do *something*. Instead of getting stuck in that outer circle, we should ask ourselves, "Why *not* me?" or "What can I do about this situation?"

On my drive home from that leadership summit, I did exactly that. I asked those two questions and I prayed for an answer and guidance. The answer I got was to start Tribe Vibe. Here's how this looked practically.

In asking myself what I could do to properly work in my circle of influence, I challenged myself to think of the last time I had been inspired—at work. I searched hard through my memories of work and what my company had offered me in the way of inspiration. Had I been inspired to excel? To spark any sort of change? To be 'all in'? I was shocked and saddened to discover that in two and a half years, I could not remember a single moment of inspiration. This got me thinking. What about the people who worked alongside me? What about the ones who weren't actively searching out inspiration, but were just as hungry, nonetheless? Surely, I wasn't the only one disheartened.

I got home and walked straight to my computer and wrote an email. I had thought of six people in the company from different divisions that I hoped would be open to what I was about to propose. The email basically went like this: Hey! I'm interested in getting people together to mutually inspire one another. Would you like to get together for lunch, watch a short inspirational Ted Talk, discuss it and share something we will DO as a result? That was it. Short. Simple. Easy, right?

I wish I could tell you that I hit send on that email immediately, but those WhatIfAbouts were hard at work. My biggest fear was not being laughed at or of people thinking this was a silly idea. My biggest fear was being ignored. *What if nobody responds? What if nobody mentions it and the reaction is just indifference?* These WhatIfAbouts kept me swimming in head trash for the rest of the weekend. Finally, on Sunday afternoon I sat back down at my computer, opened my drafts folder and hit send. It was 2 o'clock on a Sunday afternoon. I got four of six responses within an hour. All positive. All telling me they were excited and had been looking/waiting for something like this. Five of the six original invitees showed up at the first meeting. The sixth was out of town. We did exactly what the email had said we would do and Tribe Vibe was launched.

Tribe Vibe's Growth

What follows is a detailed description of what Tribe Vibe meetings looked like. I've had several people ask me about the format and flow, so I wanted to include it here.

Over a span of about nine months after that initial meeting, this group would grow by word of mouth from the original six to over 200 people. Each meeting opened with intentional networking— random groupings of members with two questions they all had to ask one another. This put everyone on the same "level of awkward" and helped break the ice. After networking, two members presented life hacks. These life hacks were anything from how to make a grilled cheese in a toaster to how to tie a dress shoe so it stays tied all day. After networking we watched a Ted Talk, huddled together in small groups and answered two questions.

1. What will you take from this personally?

2. How can you take what you learned back to your work group/team?

Each small group contained a discussion leader tasked with keeping the group on topic and on time. Group leaders were also responsible for recording the top two answers to each question to share with the larger group. Additionally, each person stated something they would DO before the next meeting as a result of their experience that day.

The energy in these meetings was electric. We covered topics from job shadowing to the "pecking order" to how to start a movement. My favorite topic was personal mission statements which became the **do** for one of the meetings. I was amazed by how many had never written a personal mission statement before. It's sad really, that so many of us can quote the corporate mission statements of the places we work from memory, but when asked about our own personal mission statement by which we lead our lives, we draw a blank. Tribe Vibe members were asked to create their own mission statement, put their name on it if they wanted, and bring it to the next meeting. At that meeting we placed the mission statements around the room for the whole group to read. One member told me this was the most difficult thing he had ever been asked to do in his twenty years in corporate America.

I'm tempted to jump up on my soap box here but let me just say this. Your work life and your OD/passion/what makes your heart come alive should be so intertwined that it's hard to tell which is which. We have been duped into believing that an intersection of these is only for the lucky. This is not the case! You can find a job or create one that brings these two parts of your life together in a powerful way. That's what I did with Tribe Vibe and then again with going full-time with Fire Starters Inc. **It's not just for the lucky.** Please believe me when I say this. Believe me because I have seen it happen in my own life. Believe me because I have seen it happen in the lives of countless members of my tribe as well the Fire Starters in this book. Another reason I was so specific in my description of Tribe Vibe is so you could replicate it where you work. Or, you could just use it as an idea starter. Whatever you decide, please, DO SOMETHING. If I can do it, you can do it.

An interesting thing happened as a result of Tribe Vibe's growth. I started sharing my dreams with other people little bits at a time— throwing teasers out there to see what people thought. To my surprise, people were excited, and they even cheered me on. They had suggestions and insight that I never would have thought up on my own. This stirred more dreaming and more sharing and more encouragement from my tribe. But, there were also days when the ember was buried under the cold, wet ashes of the WhatIfAbouts. Those days were a struggle. Remember, bringing the ember to full flame is not easy business. There were more and more days, though, when the ember turned into flame enough for it to make a lasting, nagging impression on me. Fortunately, the flame was starting to throw off some heat and people were being drawn to the flame they could see ignited in me.

I continued to meet with members of my tribe who were challenging me with questions about my dream and vision. Some had been to Tribe Vibe meetings and saw the potential. They would ask me why I wasn't speaking and getting paid for it, or why I wasn't putting myself "out there" so that I could gauge reactions to my content. Their questions fueled my fire urging me to take another small step and apply to speak at a conference or have coffee with someone who could be a potential client. Again, some were victories while others were not. I learned from both and took the next small step, and then another. And another. And another.

Tribe Vibe grew exponentially and was eventually killed by the "corporate powers" for, among other things, not being part of the 2020 vision. Another loss, in some ways, but also another step forward and another lesson learned. During all this growth, my spark had found flammable material and the flame was growing. Turns out I did have something to say and people did want to listen. One more step.

As months continued to pass, I published my website, spoke at a few conferences, posted a lot on social media, and began to embrace my OD. The result of all these little steps? Gigs around the country for which I got paid to speak for 60-90 minutes, had my travel and hotel expenses paid for, and had an absolute blast doing it. At the risk of sounding like a broken record or in case you've still not grasped it—what I am describing is not just for the lucky. It is available to you right now. You don't need to move to a new city or buy a new gadget or join a gym. You could, but they are not required to find your OD and light your fire!

You also don't need to quit your job and make some radical life altering change. I mean, maybe that's where you've landed after reading this, but again, not necessary to get started. Try a new sport.

Call an old friend and commit to doing something every month that excites you both. Volunteer at a local charity. Join a board of an organization you love. Take one small step.

When Tribe Vibe challenged members to write a mission statement, I was challenged by my tribal council to write one for Tribe Vibe in ten words or less. Here it is.

Tribe On! To challenge, inspire, connect and grow.

That's really what this book is all about. I have lived it during the three years it has taken me to write it. My Fire Starters lived it too. You can make the decision right now to discover *your* OD and light your fire. Stop waiting for permission.

One day or day one? You decide.

WHAT WILL YOU DO?

Tribe On!

ACKNOWLEDGEMENTS

This book has been a collective tribal effort by so many, but I would like to acknowledge:

Nicole Busch at Nicole Blair Wear for her book cover and branding ideas and inspiration (www.nicoleblairwear.com);

Julie Nor-Barber at Flair Studio for designing the cover (www.flairstudio.net);

Becky Fields for her masterful editing skills;

Cathy Fyock for sharing her passion about writing in an ATD workshop that awoke the author in me

Mike Bensi, Mike Vacanti, Amy Waninger, and Larry Crocker for insight, inspiration and encouragement to finish the book, plain and simple;

My tribe of supporters that subscribe to the Tribe Vibe weekly emails. Your messages have inspired and continue to inspire me to keep doing what I'm doing;

My LinkedIN and Twitter tribes for liking, sharing and commenting on my posts and helping me fan the flame and spread the word.

Tribe On!

References

Council, T. A. (2019). *Elements of Fire*. Retrieved from Smokeybear.com: https://smokeybear.com/en/about-wildland-fire/fire-science/elements-of-fire

Science Learning Hub. (2009, November 19). *What is Smoke*. Retrieved from Science Learning Hub: https://www.sciencelearn.org.nz/resources/748-what-is-smoke

Farlex, Inc. (2003-2019). *blow smoke definition*. Retrieved from The Free Dictionary by Farlex: https://idioms.thefreedictionary.com/blow+smoke

Tyndale House Publishers, Inc. (2007). *Holy Bible, New Living Translation.* Carol Stream: Tyndale House.

Tyndale House Publishers, Inc. (2007). *Holy Bible, New Living Translation.* Carol Stream: Tyndale House.

Dudley, D. (2010, September). *Everyday Leadership*. Retrieved from TED Ideas Worth Spreading: https://www.ted.com/talks/drew_dudley_everyday_leadership?language=en

Godin, S. (October 2008). *Tribes: We Need You to Lead Us.* London: Penguin Publishing Group.

Canfield, J. (2015). *The success principles: How to get from where you are to wehre you want to be.* New York: William Morrow.

Covey, S. (1989). *The 7 Habits of Highly Effective People.* New York: Simon & Schuster.

Adele. (2015, November 24). 'You Can't Prepare Yourself': A Conversation with Adele. (A. Shapiro, Interviewer)

ABOUT THE AUTHOR

Jason Barnaby specializes in igniting sustainable change in individuals and corporations. A 20-year veteran of the adult education world, he has taught in universities around the world—much of that alongside a 10-year career in the financial services industry. When that career ended in the spring of 2018, Jason jumped full time into building a business he'd been planning for over 20 years.

He is Tribe Leader and Chief Fire Starter for Fire Starters Inc.-- whose mission is to work with individuals and corporations as they challenge the barriers of fear, build a tribe of supporters and find success in their original design. Jason thrives in settings where he can be part of facilitating A-HA moments and the power that comes from those experiences. He proudly wears the Performance Index label of "Maverick" and is a 7 (or Enthusiast) on the Enneagram.

Outside of professional pursuits he is a devoted husband of 21 years, a proud father of 3, church music leader, and, along with his wife, a certified group fitness instructor.

You can see more of Jason's work on his website @

www.firestarterstribe.com

Contact Jason for conference keynotes, corporate leadership off-site workshops and individual or team coaching.

You can also sign up to Join the Tribe and receive 3 weekly emails from Jason—Monday Morning Motivation (M3) Hump Day Hacks (HDH) and Friday Freestyle.

Follow Jason on social media:

Facebook—Jason Barnaby—Fire Starter

Instagram—firestarterstribe

Twitter—Jason_Barnaby

Made in the USA
Middletown, DE
03 April 2019